CONTENTS

Acknowledgements

Text by Graham Rice
Illustrations by Russell Barnet 4-11, 24-5, 28-37, 44-5, 60-77; Gary Marsh 12-23; The Garden
Studio/Bob Bampton 26-7, 38-43, 46-9, 78-85/Rachel Birkett 86-91/Josephine Martin ⌐

First published in 1982 by Octopus Books
This edition published in Great Britain in 1995 by Chancellor Press,
an imprint of Reed Consumer Books Limited
Michelin House, 81 Fulham Road, London SW3 6RB
and Auckland, Melbourne, Singapore and Toronto

© 1982 Reed International Books Limited

ISBN 1 85152 824 5

A catalogue record for this book is available from the British Library

Produced by Mandarin Offset, Hong Kong
Printed and bound in China

GUIDE TO GOOD PRUNING

WHY PRUNE?
- To improve the shape of the plant
- To restrict the plant to a particular size
- To promote better flowering
- To encourage larger and better fruits
- To produce an abundance of attractive foliage
- To produce attractive stems
- To keep the plant healthy

SHAPE
Most shrubs look best when their natural shape is retained. In most situations the 'buns' and 'boxes' produced by over-zealous clipping should be avoided, unless, of course, you intend to practise topiary.

Shrubs that have been smothered, lost branches or are misshapen can be reshaped as follows:
1. Remove straggling branches to a lateral within the main bulk of the plant.
2. Carefully reduce the number of shoots on the 'good' side.
3. On the 'bad' side cut back weak shoots hard and strong shoots lightly.
4. Feed the plant with a good general fertiliser and mulch well.

An upright habit can be encouraged by pruning to an inward facing bud and removing spreading shoots – though this is usually less successful than pruning to an outward facing bud for spreading growth.

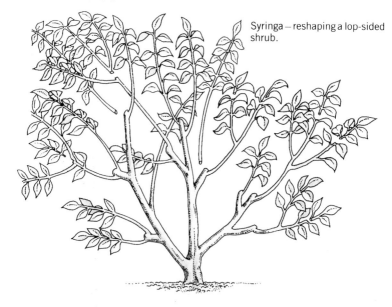

Syringa – reshaping a lop-sided shrub.

SIZE If summer flowering shrubs are cut annually to about 7.5 cm (3 in) they will never grow larger than the length of one year's growth. The same shrub could be cut back each year to a taller framework to allow for underplanting. Removing less or none of the growth made the previous year will lead to tall, ungainly specimens, with flowers at the top of spindly stems. Hard pruning usually results in a small number of vigorous shoots, while light pruning produces more less-vigorous shoots.

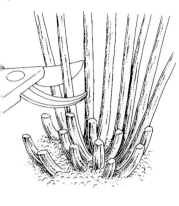

Spiraea japonica — cut down to ground level in spring.

The size of spring flowering shrubs can be controlled by cutting back the tallest branches to a bud or shoot low down on the plant. The tall stems on plants that shoot well from the base can be cut out entirely. Some plants will tolerate cutting all growth down to ground level, though one year's flowers will be lost.

Most shrubs will tolerate cutting back to near the base of the previous year's growth but some such as Calluna, Cistus, Cytisus, Erica and Genista, are liable to collapse totally if cut back harder.

Compact growth later the same year.

FLOWERS

To obtain a good floral display the growth that produces the most flowers must be encouraged. Buddleias, for example, flower on the current season's wood, which means the shoots that have grown earlier the same year. So, in order to promote good flowering, these shoots must be encouraged to make as much strong growth as possible during the season, and are cut back hard in the spring. As a result, the flowers will be twice the size of those on unpruned plants.

Other shrubs, such as Philadelphus, produce their flowers on shoots that have grown the previous year, so if these are cut hard in the spring all the flower buds will be cut off and they will not flower until the following season. These shrubs, therefore, should always be pruned *after* flowering.

Bedding plants also need to be pruned, or rather pinched back. By pinching back the central shoot of Antirrhinums to 10 cm (4 in) the plant will be stimulated into making much more bushy growth, with each side shoot producing a flower spike. For a profusion of flowers other bedding plants should be treated in the same way.

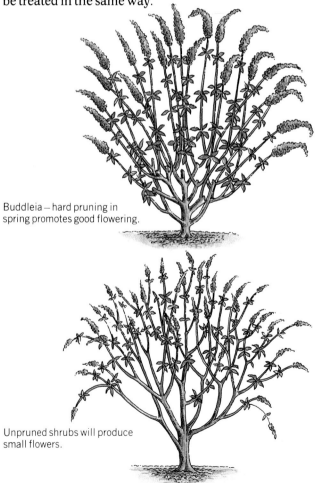

Buddleia – hard pruning in spring promotes good flowering.

Unpruned shrubs will produce small flowers.

FRUIT

Flowers ultimately lead to fruit so the same pruning guidelines apply. The aim must always be to encourage productive growth, though the method will vary with the type of crop. Vines, raspberries, peaches, apples and figs, all fruit in different ways and so need different treatment. Vines, for example, should always be pruned in winter as they may bleed to death if pruned in spring or summer.

Although large crops are the obvious aim, there can come a point when the tree bears too many fruits and their size is inevitably reduced. If the crop is thinned out the individual fruits will be much larger. An apple tree bearing large clusters of fruit irregularly spaced along the branch, will produce smaller apples than if the same number of fruits were spread more evenly along the branch.

If a shrub is grown for its ornamental fruits then the desire to retain these on the plant for as long as possible forces a change in pruning practice. Whereas pruning would normally take place after flowering, when dealing with ornamental trees and shrubs it is necessary to wait until after they have finished fruiting.

Apple
Clusters of large fruit.

Small, poor quality fruit.

FOLIAGE AND STEMS
Plants with variegated or coloured leaves can be pruned to emphasise these features, although at the expense of flowers or fruit. The Purple Smoke Bush, *Cotinus coggygria* 'Royal Purple', and the variegated Weigela, *Weigela florida* 'Variegata', are good examples. For the best foliage, these should be cut back to three or four buds once they start to grow in the spring. Evergreens should be treated less severely than deciduous subjects and should be pruned a little later.

With the variegated and yellow leaved varieties there may be a tendency to reversion – that is, the occasional green shoot may appear amongst the coloured ones. Reverted shoots are usually far more vigorous and should be cut right out at their point of origin, or gradually they will swamp the rest of the plant.

Some Dogwoods (Cornus) and Willows (Salix) are grown for their brightly coloured stems, which are a valuable contribution to the garden in the winter. The colour of the young growth is the most effective, so these shrubs should be cut back hard in early spring.

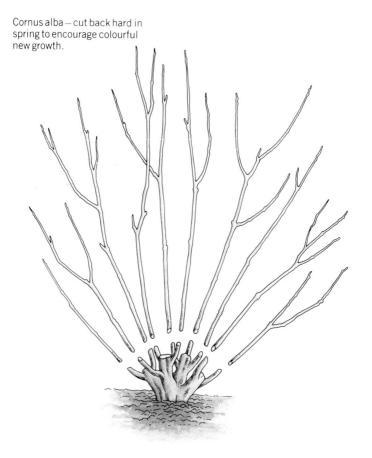

Cornus alba – cut back hard in spring to encourage colourful new growth.

KEEPING PLANTS HEALTHY

Some pests and diseases can be controlled by pruning, although it pays to be vigilant and take action before the whole plant is affected. Bad attacks can sometimes be prevented by pinching out affected growth at an early stage. Pinching out the shoot tips as soon as five clusters of flowers have formed on Broad Beans, for example, is a good method of preventing Blackfly.

The following pests and diseases can be treated by pruning:

Aphids – Greenfly, blackfly etc. – pinch out affected leaves or shoots.

Leaf miners – Cineraria and other plants belonging to the Daisy family – pick off affected leaves.

Woolly aphid – Fruit trees – cut out badly affected wood while pruning.

Black spot – Roses – remove affected leaves.

Brown rot – Apples and pears – remove all mummified fruits remaining on the tree after harvesting.

Bud blast – Rhododendron – remove affected buds.

Canker – Apples and pears – cut out infected wood.

Coral spot – Trees and shrubs – cut back to healthy wood.

Fireblight – Trees and shrubs belonging to the Rose family – cut back to healthy wood.

Powdery mildew – pinch out affected shoot tips.

Silver leaf – Cherries, almonds etc. – cut out infected wood before mid July.

Remember to burn all dead or diseased wood.

Acer (Maple) – coral spot. Cut out infected wood.

Ilex (Holly) – cut out any reverted shoots on variegated varieties.

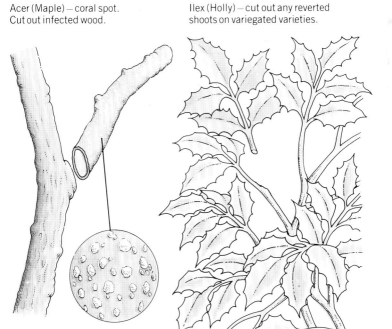

PRUNING GUIDELINES

WHAT TO PRUNE Apart from the particular pruning requirements of individual varieties, the following are common problems which can easily be solved.

Don't forget, the plant will want to grow after it has been pruned so always apply a good general fertiliser or a mulch to encourage strong new shoots.

Torn branches

Diseased wood

Rubbing branches

Canker

Crossing branches

HOW MUCH TO PRUNE

In an unpruned shoot the terminal bud produces a hormone which inhibits the growth of the lateral buds behind it. A few of these buds may grow but the leader will be far more vigorous.

If the tip of the shoot is pinched out the buds behind this, without the influence of the inhibitor, will grow out strongly. However, repeated pinching out of long shoots can produce an ungainly plant.

Harder pruning, cutting back to within 5 cm (2 in) of older wood, will stimulate the remaining buds to grow into strong shoots. Hard pruning is used when planting to encourage a bushy habit, or for summer flowering shrubs that flower on the current season's growth.

If extension growth of a leader or lateral is required, allow it to grow unchecked. Should the tip of the leader be damaged or weak, it can be cut back moderately and one of the resulting side shoots trained in to replace it. The other laterals will, of course, develop strongly.

This hard pruning stimulates this vigorous new growth.

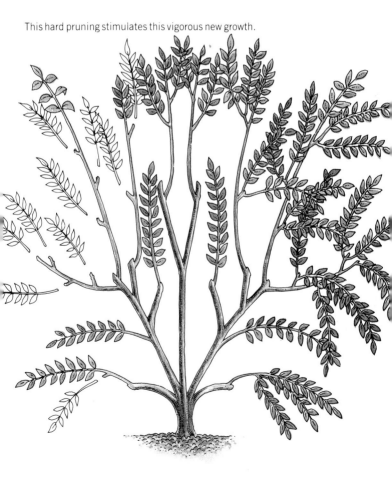

HYGIENE

When you cut a plant the exposed wood is revealed both to the air and to infection. However, as with any living thing, the plant has its own defence mechanism. The tissue just under the bark grows and becomes woody making a callus that will eventually cover the wound. Clean wounds will heal far more quickly than ragged ones which collect water and rot, so any cuts which are accidentally ragged should be recut cleanly. Stems which are squashed and split, often by the use of blunt secateurs, will also provide an entry point for disease.

Small wounds will heal quickly but those which are more than about 2.5 cm (1 in) across take rather longer, and to prevent any risk of fungal or bacterial infection these should be painted with a proprietary wound paint based on bitumen and containing a fungicide. *Don't* use gloss paint or primer. Larger wounds may take many years to heal so they should be repainted every year to maintain an efficient barrier against disease.

Clean cuts can only be made with clean tools, and these should be kept sharp and well oiled so that as little strain as possible is put on them when they are in use. Don't use secateurs to cut wire or string.

After cutting out diseased wood, avoid transferring infection to healthy growth by sterilising the saw or secateurs with methylated spirits.

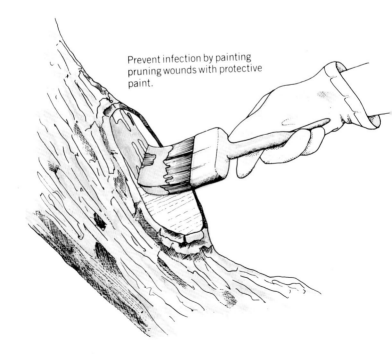

Prevent infection by painting pruning wounds with protective paint.

TIMING Never prune late in the year. In particular hard pruning towards the end of summer will stimulate soft sappy growth which may be damaged during the winter and is particularly susceptible to frost. Timing is especially crucial when it comes to encouraging maximum flower and fruit production. Any hard cutting back of plants should always be done in spring, just as they start into growth. This gives the plant a whole season in which to grow and ripen the new wood. Ripened wood is much more resistant to disease.

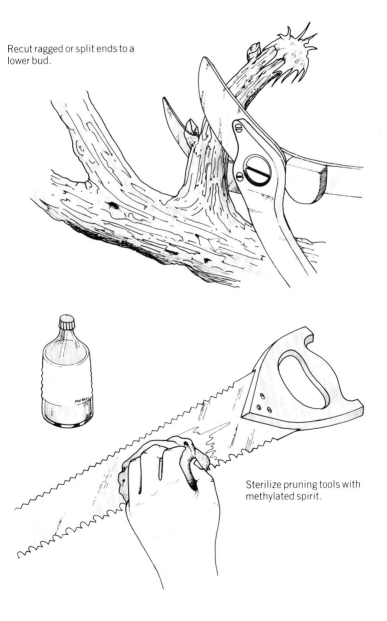

Recut ragged or split ends to a lower bud.

Sterilize pruning tools with methylated spirit.

TOOLS

Pruning tools should always be kept clean and sharp. Blunt tools are difficult to use and will also damage and bruise the shoots or branches. As with most items of equipment, buy the best tools you can afford. The initial expense will be amply repaid over the years, for good quality tools will last longer, stay sharp for longer and enable you to make cleaner cuts with less effort.

SECATEURS These are an essential piece of equipment for most gardeners. They vary in size and design but there are two main types: the anvil, with one cutting blade, and the by-pass, with two cutting blades. Before buying a pair of secateurs try them in your hand to make sure that they are comfortable and the right size, and that you can operate them easily without exerting too much pressure. The smaller models are often suitable for taking cuttings as well as light pruning.

Anvil type secateurs have a single sharp blade which cuts the wood on a flat anvil. Always place the blade *above* a bud when making a cut and do keep the blade sharp and the anvil clean. Do not twist the secateurs when cutting. With this type of secateur there can be a tendency to squash the stems, although if the blade is kept sharp this will be minimised.

A fairly recent design has a sliding, rather than a pincer-like action, and can cut thicker wood than other secateurs of the same size.

By-pass type secateurs are probably the most popular. These cut with a scissor action though only the upper blade has a cutting edge. By-pass type secateurs should be used with the slim cutting blade uppermost. One model has a swivelling lower handle which helps to prevent blistered fingers and is therefore particularly useful if you are doing a lot of pruning. The heavier models can cut wood up to about 2 cm (¾ in) thick.

- Never try to cut thicker wood than the secateurs can comfortably manage.

- Always clean off ingrained dirt, and oil the secateurs after use.

- Keep the blades closed and the catch on when the secateurs are not in use.

- Store the secateurs in a safe place out of the reach of children.

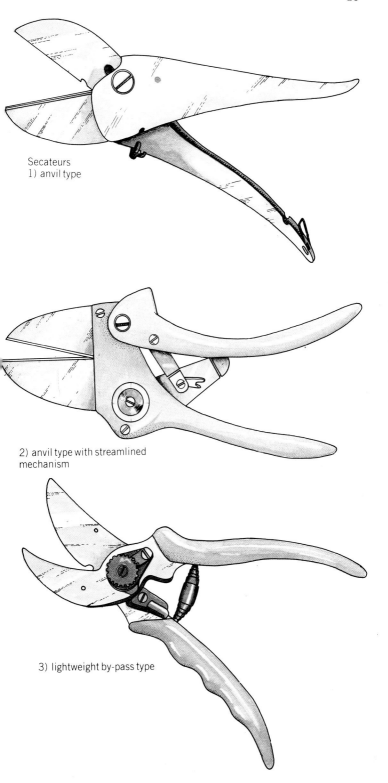

Secateurs
1) anvil type

2) anvil type with streamlined
mechanism

3) lightweight by-pass type

Long arm or long handled secateurs are useful for cutting old, hard wood which is too tough or thick for ordinary secateurs to cope with. The long handles provide extra leverage and branches up to 2.5 cm (1 in) in diameter can be cut much more easily. The long handles also give them greater reach. However, do not be tempted to wrestle with them and try and cut thick branches. This not only puts considerable strain on the tools but also makes a ragged cut.

Long loppers are simply large secateurs mounted on a very long handle (up to 3.65 m/12 ft) and operated by a wire. If you don't like ladders and heights they are invaluable for removing high branches which would otherwise be out of reach, although they are only suitable for wood up to about 2.5 cm (1 in) in diameter. A saw attachment will deal with thicker wood, though it's hard work. A fruit-gathering attachment is also available.

HAND SHEARS

These are useful for clipping small hedges, and trimming heathers after flowering to remove the dead heads. Most hand shears have a notch in the jaws for cutting heavier wood, as the blades themselves will only cut light twigs. Don't strain them by trying to cut heavier growth. A large pair of scissors can also be used to trim heathers. There are also various other types of hand clippers available, which, although operated with one hand, cut horizontally.

For very long, or tall hedges, electric clippers are a worthwhile investment, although a cheaper and useful alternative is the hedge trimming attachment for electric drills, which is very quick and efficient.

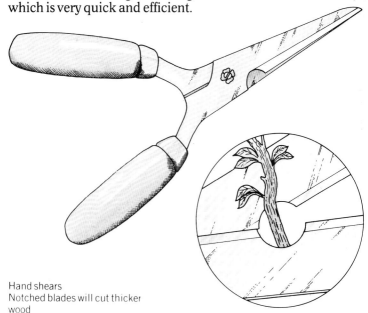

Hand shears
Notched blades will cut thicker
wood

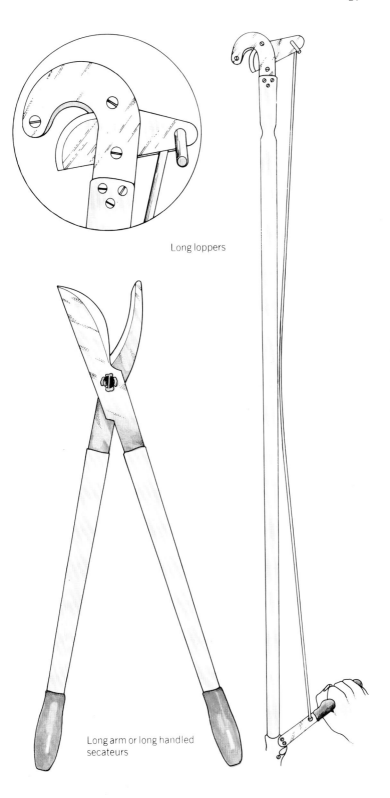

Long loppers

Long arm or long handled
secateurs

SAWS

For cutting wood which is over 2.5 cm (1 in) in diameter a saw is essential. Ordinary carpentry saws should not be used as they are not efficient at cutting green wood, and are often much too large.

Folding saw The narrow blade will cut wood up to 5 cm (2 in) in diameter, but it can be hard work on wood that is much thicker.

Grecian saw The curved blade cuts more quickly and efficiently than a straight-bladed saw.

Double sided saw The coarse teeth on one side are for live wood, and the fine teeth on the other edge for dead, dry wood. Take care not to damage branches with the side not being used for cutting.

Bow saw Sometimes called a log saw. Metal 'bow' with replaceable blades. Comes in several sizes for heavier branches.

Chain saw Electric or petrol versions are available. The greatest care should be taken when using them. This type of saw makes light work of all heavy wood but can be very dangerous if not used responsibly.

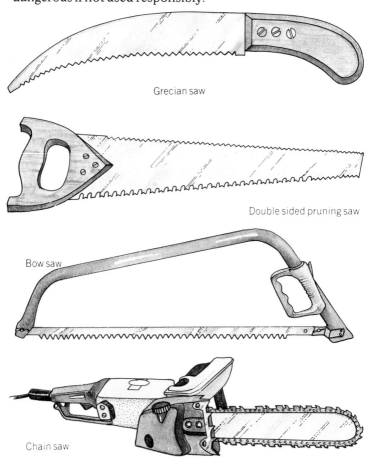

Grecian saw

Double sided pruning saw

Bow saw

Chain saw

SAFETY
Most tools can be dangerous if used wrongly, so always take care and follow the guidelines below:

- Keep all tools clean and well maintained.

- Never put equipment under undue strain, or use it for work for which it was never designed.

- Keep all tools and equipment out of the reach of children.

- Never operate electric tools in wet conditions and always use the right fuse.

- Keep power cables well away from the cutting blades when using electric tools.

- If a knife is used for pruning, keep it sharp – it is much safer to use than a blunt one.

- Never attempt to fell large trees. Leave that type of work for a qualified tree surgeon.

- Never climb into a tree to cut off branches.

- Wear gloves when pruning spiny plants.

- If you accidentally cut or graze yourself, particularly if this occurs on agricultural land, consult your doctor, who may recommend an anti-tetanus injection.

Ladders should always be securely supported.

MISCELLANEOUS TOOLS

Knives should only be used by the experienced gardener and then only with great care. They are, however, valuable for paring the edges of large saw cuts before applying protective paint.

Rope is useful when felling small trees to ensure that they fall in the right direction, and for tying in ladders.

Proprietary wound paints based on bitumen, and usually containing a fungicide, are essential to prevent infection, particularly for larger pruning cuts.

Gloves, although often scorned, are important for protecting your hands against minor cuts and grazes. Tightly stitched leather gloves are particularly useful for pruning thorny shrubs and old roses. Choose ones with long wrists to keep out thorns and other debris.

Ladders should always be well maintained. Keep the rungs free from paint and grease. When using a ladder for pruning, make sure that it is securely tied to the tree, or at least supported by another person.

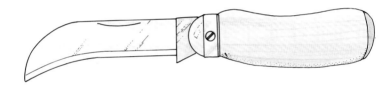

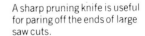

A sharp pruning knife is useful for paring off the ends of large saw cuts.

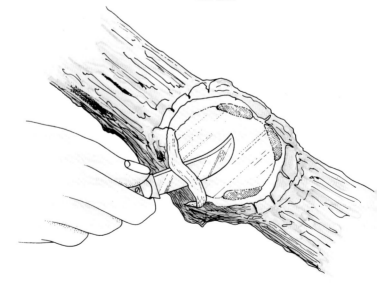

MAINTENANCE Looking after your tools will make them last longer, and perform much more efficiently.

---

1. Dirt and grime are the perfect breeding grounds for disease – to prevent the spread of infection all tools should be thoroughly cleaned after use.

2. Use emery paper to clean the grime off secateurs and to hone finely the cutting blades.

3. Protect saw blades by wiping with an oily rag after use.

4. Never leave tools out in the garden.

5. Check cables on electric tools and repair any damaged plastic coating or exposed wires.

6. Store all tools in a safe, dry place well out of reach of children.

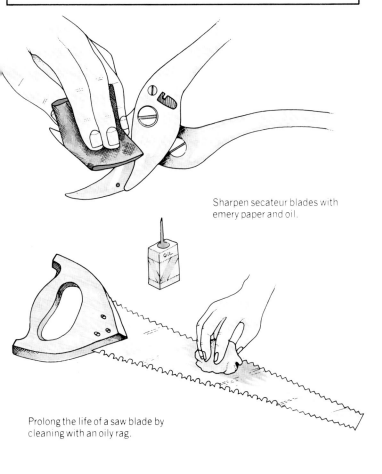

Sharpen secateur blades with emery paper and oil.

Prolong the life of a saw blade by cleaning with an oily rag.

PRUNING TECHNIQUES

HOW TO CUT There are three essential requirements for a good pruning cut:

- It should be a clean cut with no ragged edges.
- It should be just above a bud leaving no snag.
- It should slope slightly away from the bud so that water runs away from the bud.

Pruning cuts which do not fulfil these requirements are *bad* cuts and will lead to disease.

Too far from bud

Sloping the wrong way

Too close to bud

Too sharp an angle

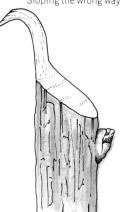
Ragged cut

Correct cut

HOW TO SAW

When removing the branch of a tree the aim should be to cut the limb cleanly and flush with the trunk or larger branch. Saw off the bulk of the branch, making an undercut first to prevent the bark from tearing. A top cut is then made a little further up the branch. The remaining stump is removed with a single cut.

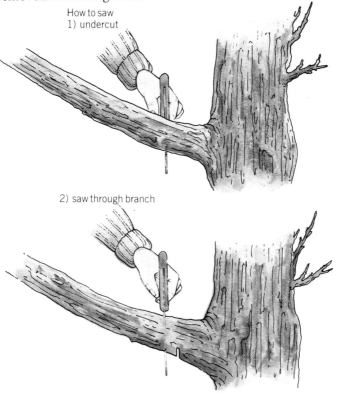

How to saw
1) undercut

2) saw through branch

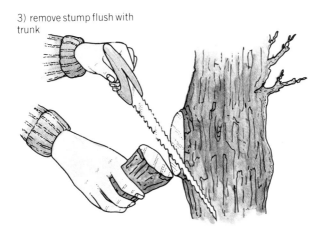

3) remove stump flush with trunk

24

MISCELLANEOUS TECHNIQUES

Rubbing out is simply rubbing off young shoots or buds which have only just started to grow, with the edge of your thumb. It is a very quick and easy way of removing unwanted shoots.

Nicking and notching are techniques which are used for training fruit trees, but are also useful for other trees and shrubs.

Notching is simply cutting out a small wedge-shaped piece of wood immediately above a bud. This notch cuts off the plant hormones from above and diverts the sap flow so that a strong shoot is produced from the dormant bud.

Nicking is cutting out a similar piece of wood from just below a bud to produce a weaker shoot.

Root pruning is sometimes used for fruit trees that have become too vigorous but it's a time-consuming job. Dig a trench about 1.5–1.8 m (5–6 ft) from the trunk, remove the soil and cut back the larger roots with a pruning saw. Do not remove the finer feeding roots. Refill the trench with soil, taking care to bury the fibrous roots at their former level. To avoid too big a check on the tree's growth, divide the operation into two halves, and root prune one side of the tree during one winter, leaving the remaining side until the following winter.

Rubbing out a bud

Notching

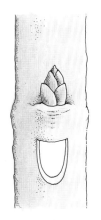

Nicking

POLLARDING is the cutting back of a tree every few years to a basic framework of branches in order to keep the head of the tree within manageable proportions. If a tree is cut back regularly to a stump-like trunk, lopping is probably the correct term. The result is unlikely to be very satisfactory as the tree's natural habit is lost. The best solution, of course, is to choose the right tree for the site in the first place, so that there is no need to continually restrict its size and habit. Cutting back Dogwoods (Cornus) to about 30–60 cm (1–2 ft) is also known as pollarding.

THE LAW

- Trees are usually protected by law and mature specimens are often placed under a preservation order.

- If your neighbour's branch overhangs your garden you may cut off the growth only on your side of the boundary.

- Any branch you cut off is still your neighbour's property and should be returned to him, especially if it has ripe fruit.

- Legally, you are liable for any damage caused by the overhanging branches of your trees if the difficulty could reasonably have been foreseen.

- If roots from a tree in your garden cause damage to your neighbour's property, he is entitled to claim compensation from you as the legal owner of the tree.

- Local authorities have the power to direct you to remove overhanging branches which obstruct the pavement. If they ask you to cut back your trees or shrubs, you should do so.

A pollarded willow tree.

PRUNING TERMINOLOGY
The parts of trees and shrubs all have particular names and it is useful to be familiar with them as it makes the description of different types of pruning so much easier.

The different parts of a shoot.

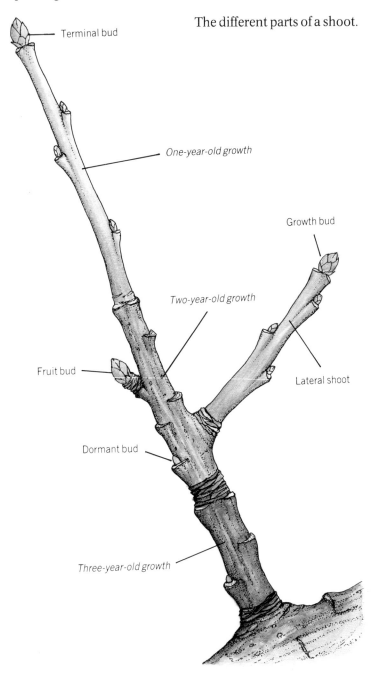

Terminal bud

One-year-old growth

Growth bud

Two-year-old growth

Fruit bud

Lateral shoot

Dormant bud

Three-year-old growth

The different parts of a tree.

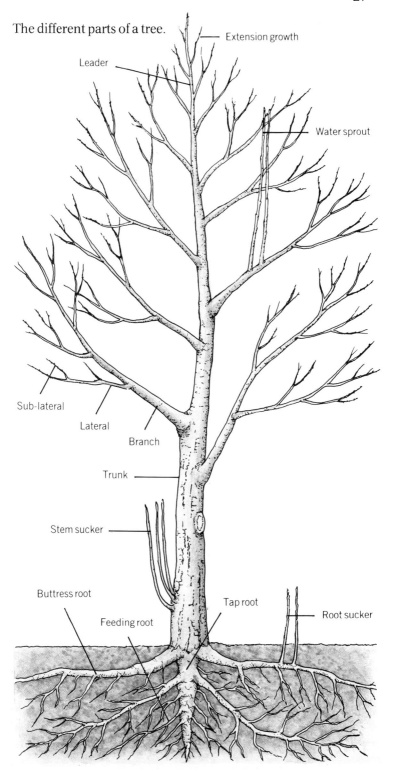

Extension growth

Leader

Water sprout

Sub-lateral

Lateral

Branch

Trunk

Stem sucker

Buttress root

Feeding root

Tap root

Root sucker

ROSES

Almost all roses need regular pruning to keep them healthy, encourage flowering and maintain their shape; all except shrub roses need to be pruned every year. The best time for pruning is undoubtedly the spring, when the roses are just starting into growth. This also enables you to put right any damage which may occur during the winter months.

PLANTING Bare-root roses are always planted during the winter when the plants are dormant. They should always be pruned *before* planting, unless, of course, this has already been done by the nurseryman. Trim back long or damaged roots and cut the tops back about 23 cm (9 in), but leave the serious formative pruning until the buds begin to shoot in spring. At this point the degree of pruning must be tailored to the particular type of rose, but most varieties are usually cut back hard during the first year. Container-grown plants, which can be planted at any time, should be pruned as usual in the spring after planting.

Cut back the shoots and roots of bare root roses before planting.

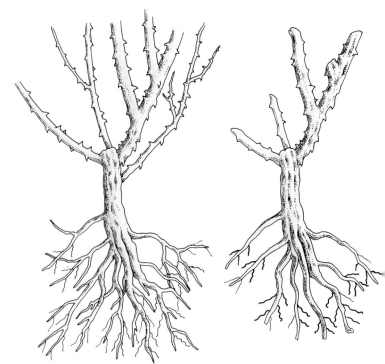

ROUTINE CARE

Flower gathering. Cutting flowers is a form of pruning and should be done properly to avoid damaging the plant. Always cut as short a stem as possible, although the actual length will largely depend on the type of flower arrangement, and always try to cut to an outward facing bud.

Dead-heading. Regular dead-heading will stimulate the production of more flowers. Single flowers of hybrid teas can be cut as they fade and then the whole head removed later. With floribundas, the whole head is removed as the last flowers finish. If shrub roses are grown for their coloured hips they should not be dead-headed. Climbers and ramblers should also be dead-headed after flowering, though this is not always easy. Towards the end of the season, dead-heading should be less severe, otherwise you will encourage light, sappy growth which will succumb to the first winter frosts.

Sucker removal. Most ornamental rose varieties are grafted on to vigorous rootstocks. Sometimes strong suckers arise from these rootstocks which would, if left, smother the plant. Always remove any suckers from their point of origin, and, if possible, tear them off. Never treat them with weedkiller.

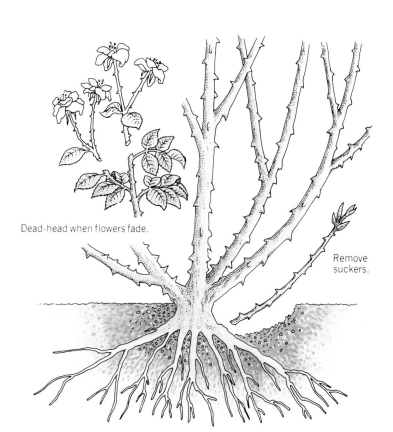

Dead-head when flowers fade.

Remove suckers.

HYBRID TEA ROSES (Large Flowered). This type of rose
tends to produce relatively small numbers of large, shapely
flowers, often with a strong scent. They flower from early June
until the arrival of severe frosts.

Choose a plant with at least three well spaced shoots, and if it
is planted during the winter or early spring cut it back in spring,
leaving two to four buds. Always try and cut to an outward
facing bud to keep the centre of the plant open. In following
years prune hybrid teas as soon as they start to grow in spring.
Cut out any dead or diseased wood which may be
distinguished by black or purple spots or patches on the bark.
Always remove any particularly weak growth since this will
probably not flower, and inward growing or crossing branches.

The ideal shape for a hybrid tea
is relatively open so that the air
can circulate freely. This helps
reduce the risk of mildew. The
remaining strong growth should
be cut back to four to six buds,
and any weaker shoots rather
harder. In later years, one or two
pieces of the oldest wood (this
has darker, rougher bark) can be
cut out at the base.

Hybrid Tea Rose
(Large Flowered)
Cut back to an outward-facing bud.

Popular Cultivars
Silver Jubilee
Grandpa Dixon
Peace
Red Devil
Wendy Cussons

FLORIBUNDA ROSES (Cluster Flowered).

This type of rose produces smaller flowers but makes up for this by carrying them in large clusters right through the summer months making a very impressive garden display.

Generally floribunda roses should be pruned less hard than hybrid teas as they are more vigorous. They make more shapely plants if they are cut back on planting to three to five buds. Choose a plant with at least three strong shoots for these will form a good framework. During the following years cut out any dead, diseased, weak or crossing shoots, and reduce the remaining shoots to six or eight buds. Cut the weaker shoots back much harder to two or three buds. In all pruning, make each cut just above a growth bud. Always remove any leaves or stems which have been blackened by frost. In later years the oldest branches can be cut out entirely.

Popular Cultivars
Iceberg
Evelyn Fison
Queen Elizabeth
City of Leeds
Southampton

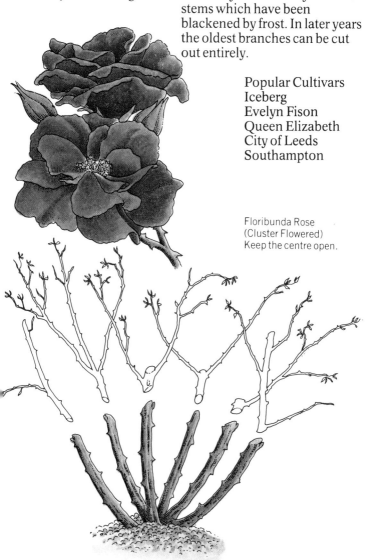

Floribunda Rose
(Cluster Flowered)
Keep the centre open.

STANDARD ROSES
Both floribundas and hybrid tea roses can be budded at the top of stems 76–122 cm (2½–4 ft) tall instead of at ground level. The main stem should be kept completely free of growth so any shoots should be rubbed out as soon as they appear. Standard roses should always be staked to prevent damage from wind, and the heads need to be kept fairly small, well balanced and open. Make each cut above an outward facing bud so that the shoots will grow away from the centre of the head. Cut back to three buds (hybrid teas) or five buds (floribundas).

WEEPING STANDARDS
These are rambler roses grafted on to 1.8–2.1 m (6–7 ft) tall stems in the same way as other standards, but the lax growth results in an attractive weeping appearance. Keep the head fairly open and well balanced. Prune by cutting out all the shoots that have flowered and retaining the previous season's growth for flowering the coming year. If this leaves too few shoots for an adequate display, a little of the old wood can be utilised by cutting back laterals to two or three buds. To help maintain the shape, tie the young shoots into a wire training frame.

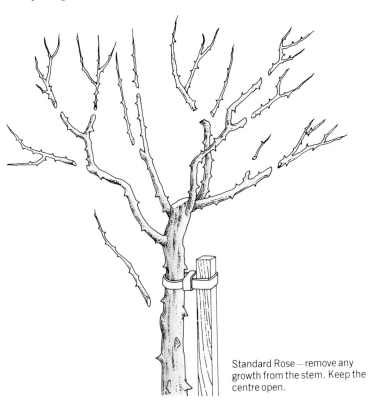

Standard Rose — remove any growth from the stem. Keep the centre open.

WIND Roses can suffer from wind damage in a number of ways so the following precautions should be taken.

- Hybrid teas and floribundas should be cut back by about half after flowering in the autumn to prevent winter winds rocking the plants and loosening the roots. Proper pruning can then follow in the spring.

- Standard roses and weeping standards should be thoroughly staked and have small symmetrical heads which are kept fairly open. In exposed gardens try and plant in a sheltered position.

- Climbers and ramblers should be tied in well to trellis, mesh or wires, otherwise the long shoots may blow down and suffer considerable damage.

- When planting roses, always make sure that the hole is large enough and that the roots are spread out evenly.

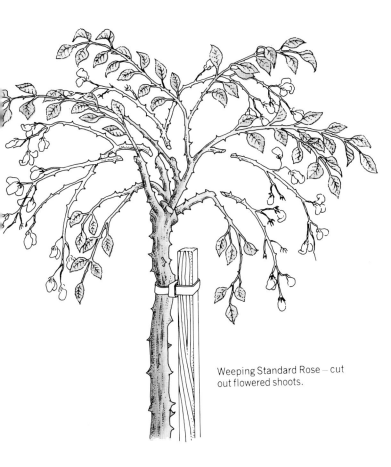

Weeping Standard Rose — cut out flowered shoots.

CLIMBING ROSES
Climbers, unlike Ramblers, will often bloom continuously throughout the summer. The aim, as far as pruning is concerned, is to build up a permanent framework of branches which are tied in securely to fence, wall or post. In the spring after planting, trim off any weak tips and small laterals before training the shoots – there should be three or four – evenly across the allotted space into a fan shape. As the new shoots grow they should also be tied in and the framework established. These branches should be retained as long as they are productive, and their laterals cut back to two or three buds every spring. Strong new shoots will appear periodically but these are usually not produced from the base; they can, though, be used to replace the oldest upper growth or to extend the framework. To encourage new growth from lower down, one of the oldest growths can be cut back hard. If the shoots can be trained horizontally this will help encourage buds towards the base to produce shoots.

Popular Cultivars
Handel
Golden Showers
Pink Perpetue
Danse du Feu
Marigold

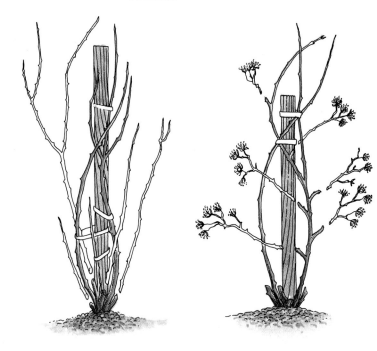

Climbing Rose – cut out old wood and reduce laterals to two or three buds.

RAMBLING ROSES

Ramblers are supple-stemmed compared with the stiff growth of climbers, and ideal for training over pillars. They are rather prone to mildew when grown against walls because of poor air circulation. They usually have only one flowering period in mid-summer, and the large trusses of flowers are born on laterals produced from the previous year's shoots. These shoots usually spring freely from the base of the plant and pruning consists of cutting out all the shoots that have produced flowers, and training in the new growth. If there are not enough new shoots then the strongest of the old ones can be retained, and the laterals cut back to two or three buds. Strong basal growth can be encouraged by feeding with a good rose fertiliser, mulching and watering well during the summer months.

Popular Cultivars	Crimson Shower
Albertine	Mme. Gregoire Staechlin
Alberic Barbier	François Juranville
Lawrence Johnston	Elegance
Easleas Golden Rambler	American Piller

Rambling Rose — cut out old wood and flowered shoots.
Tie in new growth from the base.

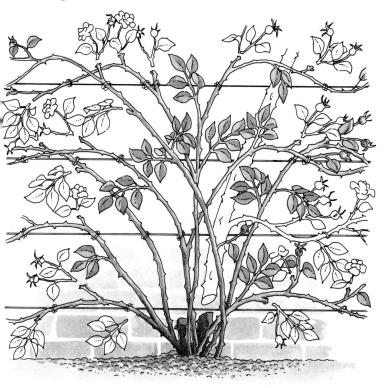

36

SHRUB ROSES There are large numbers of shrub and species roses and these could be further divided into smaller groups and different pruning methods recommended for each. Good results, though, can be had if the guidelines below are followed.

1. On planting, cut out weak and badly placed shoots and tip back the remainder.

2. Regularly dead-head all roses once the flowers have faded, provided they are not grown for their hips.

3. Concentrate on building up a strong framework of sturdy shoots. This can be steadily renewed over the years by cutting out one or two of the oldest branches at the base to leave a fairly open plant.

4. Tip back all vigorous shoots and laterals.

5. Regularly remove all weak, dead, diseased and crossing growth.

6. The species rose, *Rosa rubrifolia*, often grown for its grey-purple leaves, can be cut back fairly hard in spring if desired.

7. Always take account of the flowering habit of the plant so that pruning can be adjusted accordingly (see page 60).

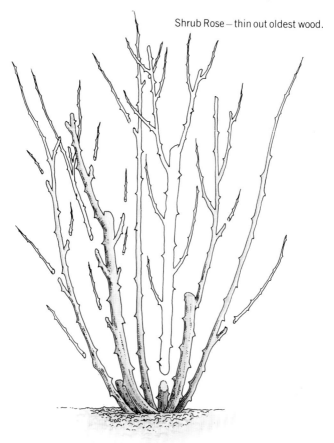

Shrub Rose – thin out oldest wood.

MINIATURE ROSES
These tiny plants usually require little pruning, but they should be trimmed back slightly on planting and any weak growth removed. Dead-heading is important in order to encourage further flowering but in spring, pruning should be relatively light, cutting back to about 15 cm (6 in), and shaping carefully.

Tender micro-roses need less pruning. A trim in spring and regular dead-heading is usually sufficient.

RENOVATION
Sometimes on taking over a new garden you will inherit roses that have been neglected for many years. In the very worst cases where there are large quantities of old wood and dead, diseased and spindly unproductive growth, the rose should be dug up and burnt. If the growth is healthy, however, though not very productive, there are two courses of action you can take.

Remove any dead or weak growth and then cut the remaining shoots back to about 5 cm (2 in) in spring. It is vital that this course of action is combined with a good feed with a rose fertiliser, followed by a generous mulch and plenty of water throughout the following summer months.

The second, more cautious approach is to cut out any dead or diseased wood. Old wood should be cut back to two thirds its length, and any new growth restricted to two buds. This procedure is continued each year until all the old wood is replaced by new. Again, feeding, mulching and watering are vital to the plant's recovery.

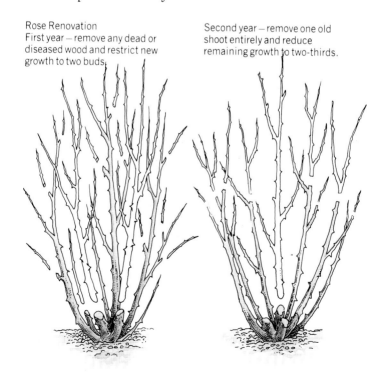

Rose Renovation
First year — remove any dead or diseased wood and restrict new growth to two buds.

Second year — remove one old shoot entirely and reduce remaining growth to two-thirds.

FRUIT – TOP FRUIT

APPLES AND PEARS The pruning requirements for apples and pears are broadly similar, although pears usually need cutting back rather harder.

Most cultivars of apples and pears produce their fruits on short lateral growths called spurs. Each spur should produce fruit for many years and the aim of the fruit grower is to produce as large a number of strong spurs as the tree can comfortably bear. Some varieties, such as Bramley's Seedling, fruit towards the tips of the previous year's shoots, and these require a different form of pruning.

The size and cropping ability of a fruit tree is determined by its rootstock, so always consult a reputable nurseryman before buying. For the best results, buy a one-year-old tree, called a maiden, and carry out the necessary training yourself.

Forming a Bush Tree and Spur Pruning Start with a tree with just one shoot and during its dormant period, cut it back to about 60 cm (2 ft). During the second year a number of vigorous shoots will be produced and these should be cut back by about half.

Follow the same procedure the following year but also cut back the laterals to three buds.

In following years, the leaders can be reduced less severely but the laterals must still be cut back to three buds. It is this

Apple – thin out overcrowded spurs

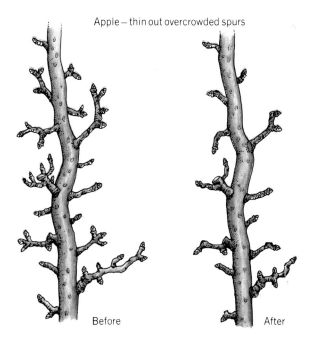

Before   After

shortening of the laterals which encourages the production of fruiting spurs.

Tip Bearers The majority of varieties respond well to spur pruning but tip-bearing types, although sometimes producing reasonable crops when pruned according to the spur system, are best if treated as follows.

Shorten the leaders by about half and cut back *some* of the shoots from the laterals to one bud, leaving the others totally unpruned so that they may bear fruit. Alternatively, as tip-bearing varieties tend to be larger, more vigorous trees, it is sometimes more convenient to simply thin out the whole tree, removing in particular any crowded or crossing branches.

The eventual aim is for an even distribution of branches with an open centre.

Tip bearers are not suitable for growing as cordons.

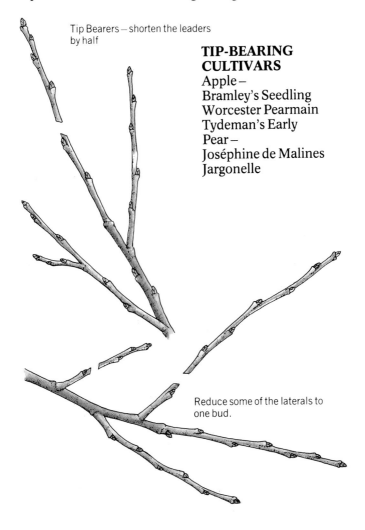

Tip Bearers — shorten the leaders by half

TIP-BEARING CULTIVARS
Apple –
Bramley's Seedling
Worcester Pearmain
Tydeman's Early
Pear –
Joséphine de Malines
Jargonelle

Reduce some of the laterals to one bud.

Cordons These are dwarf trees trained on a single stem tied to wires, and usually grown at an angle. Their small size makes them particularly convenient to look after. The fruit can be picked easily, and spraying and pruning can be comfortably carried out without a ladder. Sometimes the trees develop too many spurs, and these may need to be thinned out occasionally.

Once they are established, cordons are best pruned in the summer. In August cut back new laterals from the main stem to 7.5 cm (3 in) while sublaterals – the shoots growing from existing laterals – should be cut back to 2.5 cm (1 in). Summer pruning helps restrain the vigour of the plant, promotes the production of fruit buds and allows light to penetrate so that the fruit can ripen well.

Apple – pruning a cordon.

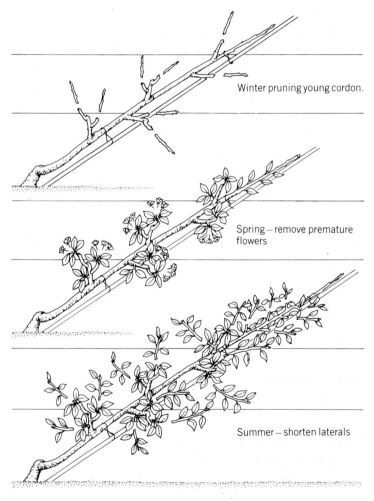

Winter pruning young cordon.

Spring – remove premature flowers

Summer – shorten laterals

Espaliers This is another form of tree with restricted growth. A central stem is trained vertically while tiers of horizontal branches are tied in to wires. Once established, espaliers are summer pruned in exactly the same way as cordons, and in the same manner overcrowded spur systems may need to be thinned in later years. Building up the framework of an espalier takes time and skill but the end result is well worth the amount of work necessary. Some nurseries sell espaliers that are already partly trained, but they tend to be rather expensive.

Apple — training an espalier.

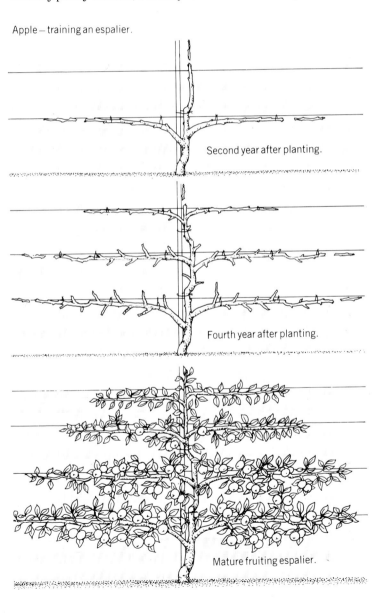

Second year after planting.

Fourth year after planting.

Mature fruiting espalier.

PLUM

This popular fruit, which also includes gages and bullaces, is normally grown as a bush, standard, half-standard or fan. Unfortunately plum trees cannot be grown as cordons or dwarf trees in the same way as apples.

The formation of a good branch structure is vital and correct training must take place in the early stages.

First winter: plant a maiden tree and cut back to 1.5–1.8 m (5–6 ft). Trim any laterals back to 7.5 cm (3 in). During the first summer, strong shoots will grow from the top of the trunk.

Second winter: choose four or five evenly spaced shoots (these will form the main branches) and cut them back by half. Shorten all other growth to 7.5 cm (3 in).

Third winter: retain two shoots on each branch selected the previous winter and cut them back by half. Cut the other shoots back to 7.5 cm (3 in).

During the following years: prune in June–July to help guard against silver leaf, a deadly fungus disease which attacks through pruning cuts in winter. Remove all dead, diseased and crossing wood. Cut back laterals to 7.5 cm (3 in). Suckers may be removed at any time.

DAMSON

Once the branch structure of these trees is established, routine pruning during June or July consists of removing any branches crowding the centre of the tree, together with any dead, diseased or unproductive wood.

Plum – remove any dead, diseased or crossing wood in June.

SWEET CHERRY

Unfortunately these trees grow very large and since two varieties are needed to ensure pollination (each tree is self-sterile), they are not recommended for small gardens. However, a new, dwarfing rootstock is becoming available and this may soon bring sweet cherries within the range of the average gardener.

The trees can be grown successfully against a wall provided there is enough space. One advantage of this method is that the crops can be protected easily from the birds with netting. Fan training is the most logical system and the framework of the tree can be built up in the same way as that given for peaches, see overleaf.

In July or August, cut out any overcrowded or badly placed branches and pinch back new growth to five leaves. Leaders can be allowed to grow if extension growth is still needed. When the space is filled cut back to a lower lateral. All shoots which grow back against the wall or strong shoots which grow forward should be cut out as soon as they appear. In the autumn all the shoots which were shortened to five leaves should be cut back to three buds. The branches should be tied into the wire during the winter months.

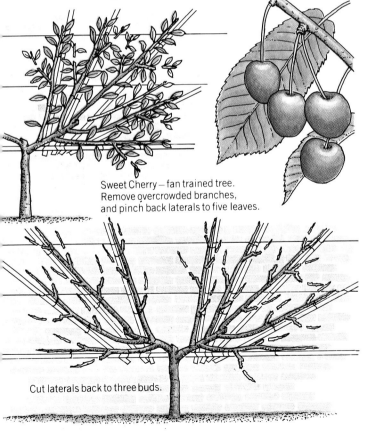

Sweet Cherry — fan trained tree.
Remove overcrowded branches,
and pinch back laterals to five leaves.

Cut laterals back to three buds.

PEACHES AND NECTARINES
Because these trees flower early it is the blossom, rather than the plants themselves, which is tender. To help protect these fragile blooms, peaches and nectarines are usually grown against a south-facing wall or fence.

Pruning is not simple. First build up the framework of a fan trained tree. Both trees fruit on the previous year's growth so the aim is to produce a constant supply of new growth. Shoots that have fruited are removed and replaced with the new shoots which will fruit the following year.

In spring, as the buds burst, select two buds towards the base of the previous year's growth to form the fruiting shoots for next year. Rub out any buds below these.

Allow the terminal bud to produce six leaves then pinch it back to four. As the fruits swell, thin them to about 23 cm (9 in) apart.

Pinch back all shoots where there are fruits to two leaves, and the others to about 2.5 cm (1 in). Select which of the two basal shoots is best placed in relation to other branches, and cut out the other.

After fruiting, cut the branch that has fruited back to its replacement.

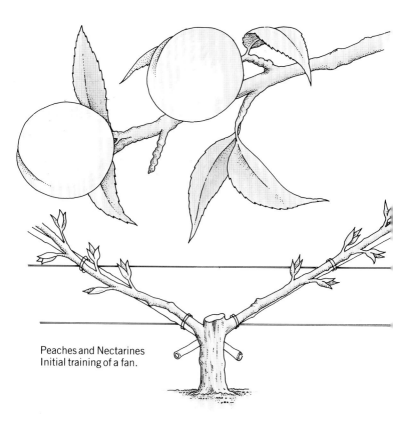

Peaches and Nectarines
Initial training of a fan.

MORELLO CHERRY

These fruit in much the same way as peaches and if trained as a fan tree can be pruned in a similar way. Some varieties do not produce strong replacement shoots readily, so a proportion of the older growth may need to be cut back hard. Morellos can also be grown as ordinary trees in the same way as plums, in which case pruning consists of cutting older shoots back to one-year-old laterals in spring. If there are only a few laterals some of the previous year's shoots may need to be cut back to 7.5–10 cm (3–4 in) as well.

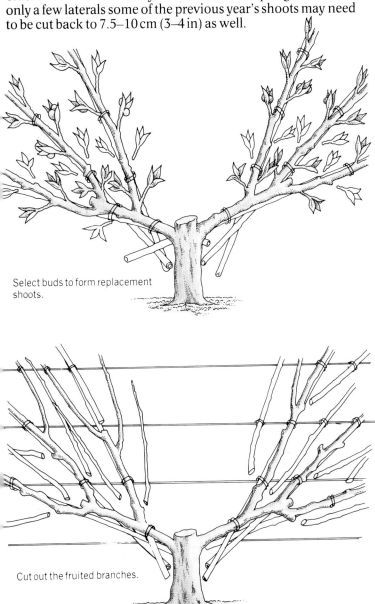

Select buds to form replacement shoots.

Cut out the fruited branches.

FIG Although they can be grown successfully as bush trees, figs are much more likely to crop well if given the added warmth of a south-facing wall and trained as a fan. They are very decorative plants and valued for their foliage alone.

Young figs develop in late summer on the tips of short laterals produced earlier in the year. The fruits remain on the plant over the winter to ripen during the following summer. As the figs ripen, more young fruits appear on new shoots, but if the summer is not hot enough to ripen these, too, they are best removed.

Unless the roots are restricted, fig trees will need root pruning once they are seven years old, and again at two-yearly intervals. Routine pruning procedure is simply to cut the shoots that have fruited back to one or two buds in spring. At the same time cut out any overcrowded branches leaving the remaining branches about 23 cm (9 in) apart. Also remove any suckers and frost-damaged wood. In late June cut back young growth to five buds. Next year's fruits will form on the resulting laterals.

Plants grown solely for ornament, especially if grown in pots, can be cut back hard in spring.

Fig – cut back young growth to five leaves.

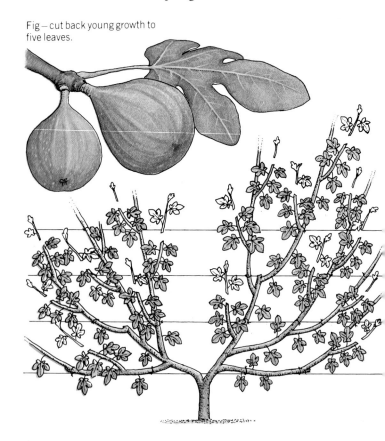

OTHER FRUITS

Cobnuts and filberts In larger gardens, especially if there are no squirrels in the surrounding area, nuts can be grown successfully. Routine pruning is fairly straightforward. Remove all suckers with a sharp knife, and keep the centre of the tree open by cutting out any crowding branches in early spring. Laterals can also be cut back to a flower bud, when the catkins are open.

Quince Thin out three- or four-year-old wood every year to keep the bush open.

Medlar Reduce terminal growths by half during the first four years. Remove any weak or badly positioned branches in order to keep the centre open on mature trees.

Walnut If you have enough space to plant a walnut, young trees can be induced to fruit earlier than usual by pinching back the shoots. Aim to build up an open, regular-shaped head but in the third July after planting, pinch out the tips of the vigorous shoots – not the thin ones with the catkins – after the fifth leaf. Repeat this same procedure for the next five years to encourage the trees to fruit on the lower parts of the shoots. Do not prune walnut trees between November and May.

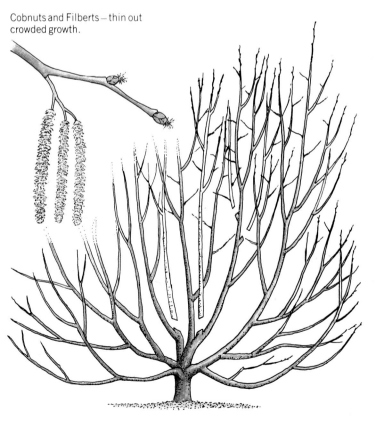

Cobnuts and Filberts – thin out crowded growth.

RENOVATION

Sometimes, especially when moving to a new house, one inherits a tree that has been badly neglected. This usually means that it is totally unpruned and probably starving as well. If the tree is old and very badly diseased the best solution is to remove it and to plant a new one, preferably in a different spot.

If, however, you think you can save the tree, proceed as follows:

1. Remove all grass and weeds from around the base of the trunk. Apply a good general fertiliser, mulch well and water as necessary.

2. Over the next one to three years, depending on the size of the tree, remove the older branches, leaving an open framework of the healthiest wood. Prune apples and pears in winter, plums and cherries in summer.

3. Stake the tree if necessary.

4. Thin out any fruiting spurs that have become overcrowded.

5. Remove any suckers from the base and stem.

6. Remember to paint all pruning wounds with a protective sealing paint containing a built-in fungicide to guard against the risk of infection.

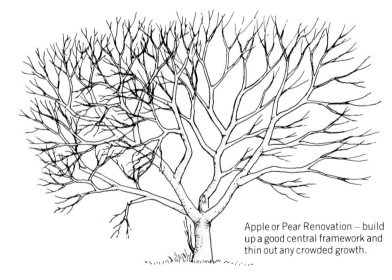

Apple or Pear Renovation — build up a good central framework and thin out any crowded growth.

DISEASES OF FRUIT TREES AND BUSHES

A number of fungal and bacterial diseases that attack fruit trees can be controlled by pruning.

Cankers of apples, pears, plums and cherries can be treated without removing the branch if they are small. Simply cut away all the infected areas and paint with wound paint. In severe cases it may be necessary to remove the whole branch. Always paint the wound to seal it against further infection.

Silver leaf and **fireblight** affected wood should be cut back to healthy tissue.

Coral spot. Any dead wood infected with this disease should be removed promptly or the infection may spread to live, healthy wood.

Gall mite, or 'big bud' mite as it is sometimes called, infects the buds of black currants, causing them to swell to about double their normal size. If you act quickly, the attack can be controlled by picking off the affected shoots.

Leaf curl damages the shoots of plums, cherries and peaches. Pinch out infected shoots.

Remember to burn all dead or diseased wood.

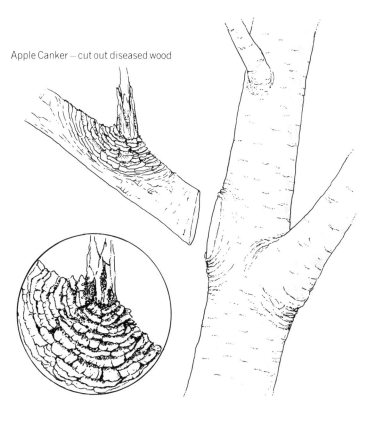

Apple Canker — cut out diseased wood

SOFT FRUIT

RASPBERRY This has a characteristic habit of growth which is shared by blackberries and loganberries. Instead of forming a basic branch structure that persists from year to year, strong growths are made each year from below ground, so unless regular pruning is carried out each year, the result is an impenetrable and sparsely fruiting thicket.

Summer fruiting raspberries produce fruit on short laterals from the canes produced during the previous year. Autumn fruiting varieties produce raspberries on the current season's growth. Always plant canes which are certified virus-free. Plant new canes about 60 cm (2 ft) apart during the winter months

Raspberry – cut out old canes after fruiting.

and cut them down to 23 cm (9 in). New shoots will appear in the spring and when these are growing well the old cane stumps can be removed completely. Tie the canes to horizontal wires as they grow.

Make sure all the canes are tied in well by the winter, and in the spring cut the tips back to 15 cm (6 in) above the top wire. Laterals will be produced during the spring which will flower and fruit, and at the same time strong new shoots will appear from the base. Select enough to provide one cane every 7.5–10 cm (3–4 in) and remove the others. After fruiting, all the canes that have produced a crop should be cut out at ground level and the new canes tied in.

Autumn fruiting varieties should be cut down to 23 cm (9 in) on planting, and cut down to ground level each spring. During late spring, thin out the weakest shoots leaving the strongest canes to grow on.

Cut autumn-fruiting varieties to ground level in spring.

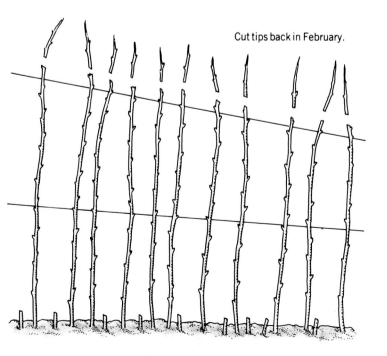

Cut tips back in February.

BLACK CURRANT

When you buy your first black currant bush you need to be brave, for having planted it, in winter or early spring, you must cut the branches back very hard, leaving only 2.5–5 cm (1–2 in) with no more than two buds. (However, the healthy young shoots can be used as cuttings, so all is not lost.) During the following year these buds will produce vigorous shoots which will form the basis for future crops. If the shoots are pruned less severely on planting, or worse still, if they are not pruned at all, a large amount of weaker growth will be made, and this is the last thing you need if you want the bushes to produce good, heavy crops.

Black currants fruit on shoots that have grown during the previous season, so although weak new shoots can be cut out at the base, the others should not be pruned at all. These shoots will fruit the following summer.

In the following years, pruning consists of removing about one half to a third of the oldest wood each year, as low down on the plant as possible. Weak twigs and damaged or diseased wood should also be cut out, together with any particularly low branches from which the fruit may rub on the ground and become damaged.

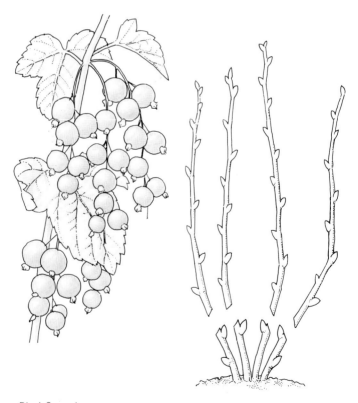

Black Currant
—cut back hard after planting.

At some time or other, black currant bushes may become infected with the black currant gall mite. This is a particularly unpleasant garden pest as there are two ways in which it affects the plant. The gall mite itself feeds and breeds in the buds of the black currant which become round, fat and unproductive. The black currant crop therefore is much reduced.

Even more insidious is the fact that the gall mite carries a disease called reversion virus which not only dramatically reduces the crop but is, unfortunately, incurable. The best method of prevention is to spray with lime sulphur. The swollen infected buds are easily distinguished from the normal buds which are oval and pointed. Infected buds should be picked off and burnt as soon as they are seen. If the whole bush is affected it should be dug up and burnt. Do not replant healthy black currant bushes on the same ground.

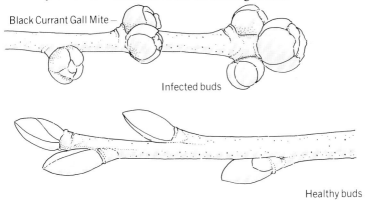

Black Currant Gall Mite —

Infected buds

Healthy buds

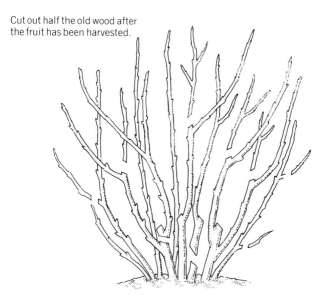

Cut out half the old wood after the fruit has been harvested.

RED AND WHITE CURRANTS

Both these fruits can be grown on short legs, as cordons or even as a dividing hedge between the fruit and vegetable garden. Red and white currants fruit on short spurs borne on the previous season's wood. When pruning, the aim should be to construct a strong spur system. In the early years build up a framework of between eight and ten permanent branches. The fruiting spurs can be encouraged to form by shortening all laterals to five leaves in summer, and in winter by cutting back the leaders by about half. As the plant matures the leaders will have to be cut back even more, and eventually reduced to 2.5 cm (1 in). The oldest dark wood can be cut back hard and new shoots from low down should be trained in to take its place. Unfortunately red and white currants suffer from gall mite and reversion virus in the same way as black currants.

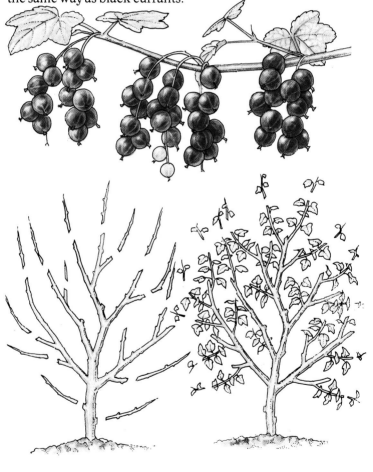

Red and White Currant — cut back the leaders by half, and the laterals to two buds.

Shorten resulting growth to five leaves.

BLACKBERRY

BLACKBERRY The cultivated varieties bear much bigger and sweeter fruits than the wild blackberries found in the hedgerows. Blackberries fruit on laterals growing from shoots made the previous year. Other related fruits which are pruned in the same way include the loganberry, boysenberry, Japanese wineberry, thornless loganberry and veitchberry.

Young blackberry plants should be cut back to 23 cm (9 in) when planting in the winter. The training in future years should stem from the fact that most blackberries are both vigorous and thorny, and if each year's growth can be kept separate it will help enormously. Blackberries should be trained on supporting wires with all the new growth trained along the wires to one side of the root only. Any damaged tips on these shoots can be lightly tipped back in early spring. These canes are the ones which will bear fruit, and at the same time a new crop of canes will appear from the base – these should be trained along the wires in the opposite direction.

After fruiting the old canes are cut out at the base and so it goes on, alternating pruning from one side to the other.

Blackberry – cut out the old canes immediately after fruiting.

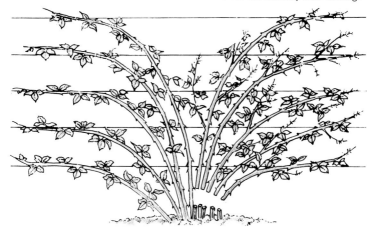

GOOSEBERRY Many people are reluctant to prune

gooseberries – possibly because of the thorns – and the result is
a tangled mass of growth with fruit that is almost impossible to
pick without getting badly scratched. Building up a sturdy
branch structure with many fruiting spurs and adequate space
between the branches is probably the best way to get good
crops of fruit which can be picked in relative comfort. Plant
between November and February when the bushes are
dormant. Cut back the side shoots by about half. As
gooseberries have a tendency to 'flop' cut to an inward facing
bud. During the following winter, select about six shoots to
form the branch structure, and cut these back by half. The
remaining shoots can be cut back to 7 cm (3 in). Continue in

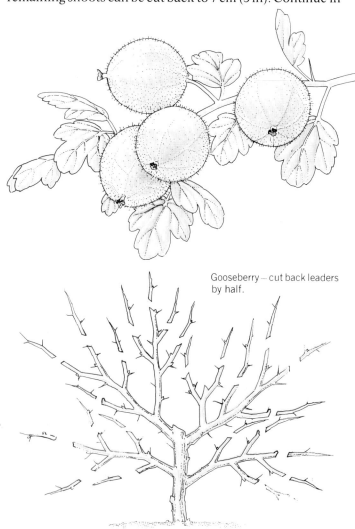

Gooseberry – cut back leaders
by half.

this manner each winter reducing the leaders by half and cutting back the laterals to 7 cm (3 in).

Summer pruning can help to produce more fruit buds and also allows the sunlight to hasten the ripening process. Simply remove the top third of all shoots – leaders and laterals – in July.

Gooseberry mildew is a particularly debilitating disease which can attack the young shoots during the summer months. If an attack of mildew is left unchecked the disease will spread to the fruits which will then be inedible. Gooseberry mildew will also infect older shoots where it will overwinter ready for reinfection the following year. So, even if you don't prune comprehensively, each summer pinch off and burn any shoot tips showing signs of mildew.

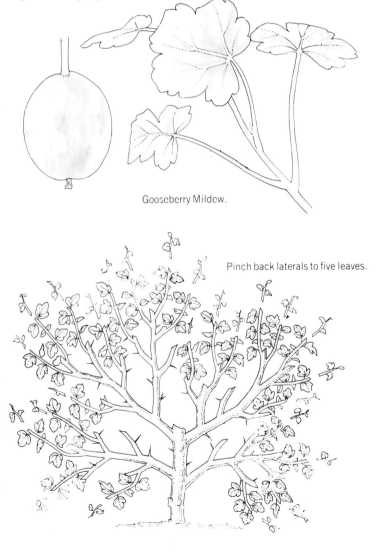

Gooseberry Mildew.

Pinch back laterals to five leaves.

VINES
With the increasing popularity of home-made wines, more and more people are growing outdoor vines and there are a number of commercial vineyards throughout the southern part of the country.

There are numerous systems for pruning and training grapes, and in some quarters it is considered quite a science. However, the following is a simple method to follow. Plant the young vine during the winter months, if possible on a south-facing slope which has some protection from spring frosts. Cut all growth back to about 15 cm (6 in). Allow one shoot to grow vertically during the following year and pinch any other growths back to one or two leaves. Late next winter cut the vine back to the bottom wire, about 38 cm (15 in), and during the following summer, train three shoots vertically, tying them in to the supporting wires. All other growth should be pinched out. In the autumn two shoots are trained out horizontally along the wires and in late winter the vertical shoots are cut to three buds.

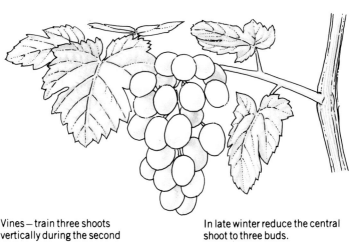

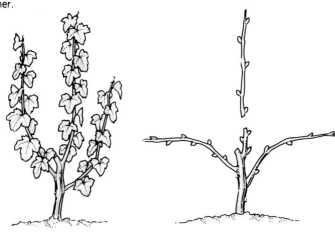

Vines — train three shoots vertically during the second summer.

In late winter reduce the central shoot to three buds.

During the summer laterals will develop from the horizontal branches, and these must be trained vertically until they reach three leaves above the top wire when they should be pinched out. These are the shoots that will bear fruit. Any sublaterals should be pinched to 2.5 cm (1in). The three buds on the short central shoot will also grow out and these should again be trained in vertically. In winter all growth except the three central shoots is cut out and this procedure is repeated every year. Always prune vines in winter as they will bleed if pruned later.

Indoor vines Grapes in the greenhouse are usually grown as single cordons. When established, the laterals are cut back to two buds each December and the leader reduced by half until it has reached its full extent when it, too, is cut hard back. During the spring, laterals are thinned to about 15 cm (6in) and tied in to supporting wires. Fruiting shoots are stopped two leaves beyond the fruit, and after fruiting is over are cut back by half.

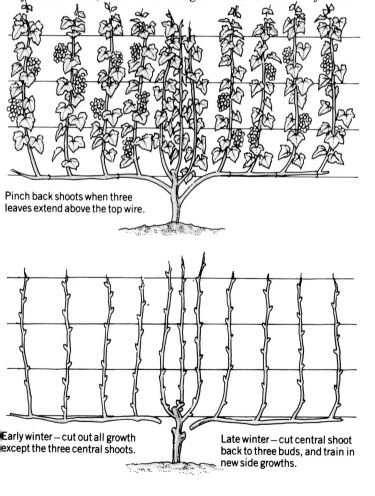

Pinch back shoots when three leaves extend above the top wire.

Early winter – cut out all growth except the three central shoots.

Late winter – cut central shoot back to three buds, and train in new side growths.

SHRUBS

Shrubs flower on *three* different types of shoot and, as far as pruning is concerned, each group is treated differently. The first group of summer-flowering plants, such as Buddleia, Caryopteris and Fuchsia, produce their flowers on growth made in the earlier part of the same year, also referred to as the current season's growth. They are pruned in late winter or early spring to encourage strong new growths to shoot from just below the pruning cut, and these shoots flower later in the year.

The second group of plants flower on the shoots that have grown during the previous year, which is also referred to as the previous season's wood. These include Forsythia, Philadelphus (Mock Orange) and Weigela. Unlike the first group, these shrubs must *not* be pruned in late winter, as the wood you would be cutting out is that bearing all the flower buds. The shrubs in this group are pruned *after* flowering. Once the flowers fade, cut out all the shoots that have borne flowers.

The third, and much smaller group, includes Chaenomeles (Japanese Quince) and Wisteria which flower, iike apple trees,

Caryopteris — prune hard in spring.

on spurs. That is, the flowers are produced from the same short, stubby growths every year. These spurs can be encouraged by shortening new growth in summer, and nipping back the resultant side shoots later in the year. Some shoots can be retained to increase the size or improve the shape of the plant.

Not all shrubs require annual pruning, so check the individual requirements of each plant before you start.

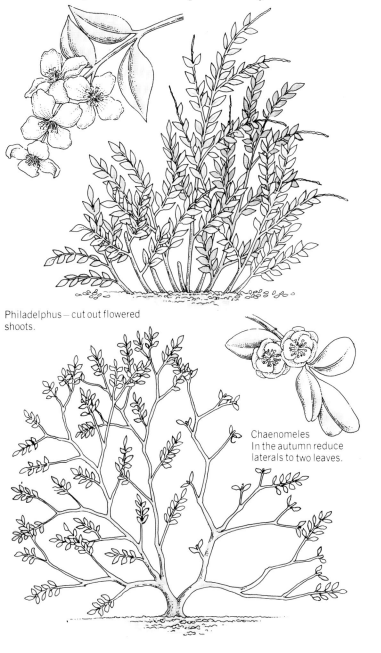

Philadelphus — cut out flowered shoots.

Chaenomeles
In the autumn reduce laterals to two leaves.

SHRUB GUIDE

AUCUBA
Never clip with shears as the leaves die if cut. To shape, or rejuvenate old plants, cut back hard in spring.

BERBERIS (BARBERRY) (2)
No regular pruning required. Deciduous varieties can be thinned in July to prevent thickets becoming too dense. Prune evergreen varieties after flowering. If you want to retain the berries, these shoots can be cut out the following year.

BUDDLEIA (BUTTERFLY BUSH) (1)
B. davidii, the common type, should be cut back hard in spring. Prune *B. globosa* (with round, orange flower heads) immediately after flowering. If necessary thin out the shoots of *B. alternifolia*, and remove flowered growth after flowering.

CALLUNA (LING, HEATHER) (1)
Clip with shears in spring to keep the plants bushy.

CAMELLIA (2)
Normally little pruning is needed though dead flowers can be removed. To shape, cut back hard in spring and feed well.

CARYOPTERIS (1)
Cut back to within 2.5 cm (1 in) of the older wood in spring.

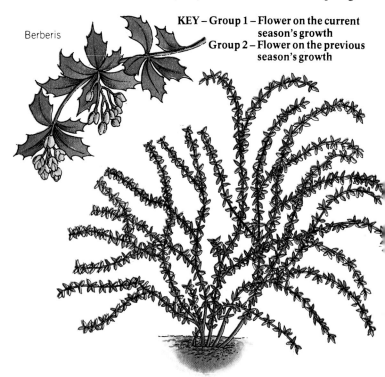

Berberis

KEY – Group 1 – Flower on the current
season's growth
Group 2 – Flower on the previous
season's growth

CEANOTHUS (CALIFORNIAN LILAC) (1 & 2)
Prune evergreen species after flowering. Cut shoots that have flowered back to two buds. Deciduous types flower on the current season's growth so cut back hard in spring.

CHOISYA (MEXICAN ORANGE) (1 & 2)
No regular pruning required. Cut back faded flowers to within 15–23 cm (6–9 in) of stem to encourage second flowering.

CISTUS (SUN ROSE)
No pruning required. Older plants will not respond to hard cutting. Dead-head after flowering.

CORNUS (DOGWOOD) (2) See page 8.

COTINUS (SMOKE TREE) (1) See page 8.

COTONEASTER (2)
No regular pruning required. Older straggly plants can be cut hard in early (deciduous varieties) or late (evergreen varieties) spring.

CYTISUS (BROOM) (2)
As the flowers fade cut the young wood back by about three quarters. *Never* cut back into older growth. *C. battandieri* can be thinned if necessary in spring.

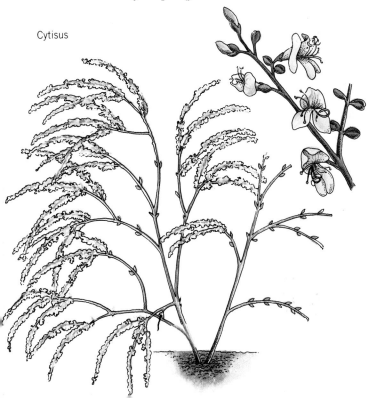

Cytisus

DAPHNE (1)
No regular pruning required. Shorten straggly growths on
D. mezereum after flowering, especially if the plant is becoming
leggy. Shape evergreen varieties after flowering if necessary.

DEUTZIA (1)
Cut out any shoots that have flowered immediately after
flowering. Remove one or two of the older shoots at the base to
make way for strong basal growth.

ELAEAGNUS (1 & 2)
Cut deciduous varieties back hard in spring. Shape evergreens
in late spring. Cut out reverted shoots of variegated varieties.

ERICA (HEATH, HEATHER) (1)
Winter and spring flowering types should be pruned after
flowering, removing most of the previous year's growth.
Summer flowering varieties should be clipped in early spring.

ESCALLONIA (1)
No regular pruning required although branches that have
flowered should be removed once the flowers fade. The shrub
can be cut back hard in spring if in need of rejuvenation.

EUCALYPTUS (GUM TREE)
Hardy species should have a single leader and branches should
be cut only if required for floral decoration. Regular cutting
back in May – after the danger of severe frosts has passed but
before the new growth begins – will produce the best foliage.
Tender species in tubs should be cut back hard each spring.

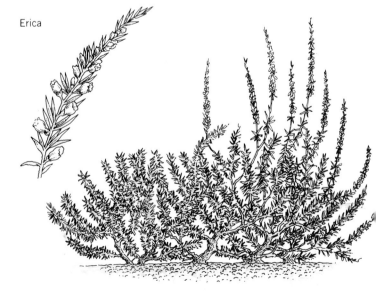

Erica

EUONYMUS (SPINDLE TREE)
These popular evergreens may be shaped up in April but
should not be clipped. Cut out any reverted shoots. Deciduous
species can be hard pruned in spring if necessary.

FATSIA (1)
No regular pruning needed although a general tidying in April
is sometimes necessary, especially after a hard winter.

FORSYTHIA (2)
Regular hard pruning will lead to soft growth but few flowers,
so after flowering cut out any old wood low down on the plant
to make room for strong shoots from the base.

FUCHSIA (1)
Hardy fuchsias are often cut down to ground level by winter
frosts, but if not they should still be cut back hard. Do not be
afraid of cutting into live wood.

GENISTA (BROOM) (2)
No regular pruning required. Shoots that have flowered should
be cut back hard as the blooms fade, but it's unwise to cut back
into old wood.

GRISELINIA
No regular pruning required. Trim out frost-damaged shoots in
April and shape if necessary.

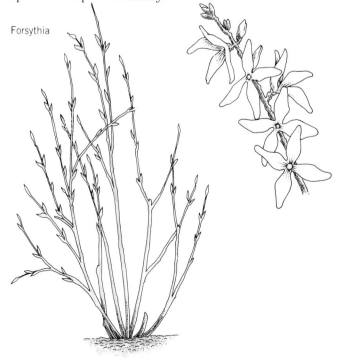

Forsythia

66

HAMAMELIS (WITCH HAZEL) (2)
Cut back any straggly growths and remove any suckers from below ground level.

HEBE (1)
The large flowered hybrids shoot well from old wood, so they can be cut back hard in spring if necessary. Shorten the previous year's shoots to keep the plant bushy. Smaller, spring flowering types can be trimmed after flowering if necessary.

HELIANTHEMUM (ROCK ROSE) (1 & 2)
Clip over after flowering to encourage further blooms in the autumn. Remove any dead shoots under the mat of live growth.

HERBS
Most herbs are at their most potent just as they are about to flower, so this is the time to cut them for drying. Sometimes a later cut is possible – thyme and sage usually produce enough growth – but large-scale cutting should not be done after August as the shoots must have time to ripen before winter. Isolated sprigs for using fresh should be cut just above the base of the current season's growth.

Helianthemum

HIBISCUS (1)
No regular pruning is necessary. This shrub is rather prone to die-back, so remove any dead wood in spring. Any long shoots should be shortened after flowering.

HYDRANGEA (2)
The large flowered *H. macrophylla* type should be dead-headed in spring and the weakest shoots cut out at ground level. *H. paniculata* can be cut back to two buds each spring.

HYPERICUM (ST JOHN'S WORT) (1)
Shrubby types can be cut back to ground level in April. *H. calycinum*, grown for ground cover, can be trimmed with shears in March.

JASMINUM (JASMINE) (2)
J. nudiflorum, the winter jasmine, should be pruned after flowering, cutting out most of the shoots that have flowered. Untidy plants can be cut back hard, within 5–7.5 cm (2–3 in) of the base.

KERRIA (JEW'S MALLOW) (2)
After flowering, cut old canes back to ground level to encourage plenty of new growth.

Hydrangea

LAVANDULA (LAVENDER) (1)

In spring remove most of the previous year's growth. Trim off faded flower spikes in late summer.

LEYCESTERIA (1)

L. formosa produces strong new shoots from the base each year and these should be cut back hard in the spring to encourage the new growth. Shorten old wood by half if necessary.

LIGUSTRUM (PRIVET) (1)

Once a framework has been established, varieties with coloured leaves can be cut back hard in spring.

MAGNOLIA (2)

No regular pruning necessary. If the shape must be improved, cut out the offending branches in July and paint the wounds. When dead-heading, the flowers should be cut not broken off.

MAHONIA (2)

M. aquifolium can be cut back after flowering to restrict its size. *M. japonica* and other tall varieties may be cut back by half when growth becomes too lanky. Do this over two seasons, preferably in spring after flowering.

OLEARIA (DAISY BUSH) (1 & 2)

Remove frost damaged shoots in April. Lightly prune spring flowering varieties when flowers are over, and summer flowering varieties in May.

Lavandula

OSMANTHUS (2)
Trim spring flowering varieties after flowering. Later flowering varieties can be cut in May.

PERNETTYA (2)
Remove the oldest wood occasionally and also any tall straggly shoots that destroy the overall shape.

PHILADELPHUS (MOCK ORANGE) (2) See page 6.

PHLOMIS (JERUSALEM SAGE) (1)
Remove frost-damaged shoots in spring and cut back old growth moderately. Do not cut into the oldest wood.

PIERIS (2)
Remove any frost-damaged or straggly shoots in spring, and dead-head after flowering. Can be cut back into old wood.

POTENTILLA (CINQUEFOIL) (1)
For shrubby species cut out any weak shoots in spring and reduce the previous year's growth by about half.

Pernettya

PYRACANTHA (FIRETHORN) (2)
No regular pruning necessary for plants grown as free-standing bushes. For plants trained on a wall as a fan, cut back any shoots growing away from the wall after flowering

RHODODENDRON (2)
Both Rhododendrons and Azaleas should be dead-headed if possible and any buds affected by bud blast should also be removed. If necessary, cut back any straggling shoots after flowering. Overgrown specimens can be cut hard when the flowers fade.

RIBES (FLOWERING CURRANT) (2)
Shoots which have flowered can be cut back to a good replacement shoot and some of the oldest wood cut back hard.

ROSMARINUS (ROSEMARY) (2)
Any frost-damaged growth should be removed in spring and the plants can be trimmed into shape after flowering.

SANTOLINA (COTTON LAVENDER) (1)
Trim after flowering or the bushes will sprawl untidily, revealing a bare centre. If grown for their foliage only, trim hard in April. Unpruned plants are generally short-lived.

SENECIO (1)
Remove the faded flower stems together with any long straggly shoots. Cut back hard in spring if necessary. Do not cut hedging forms with shears.

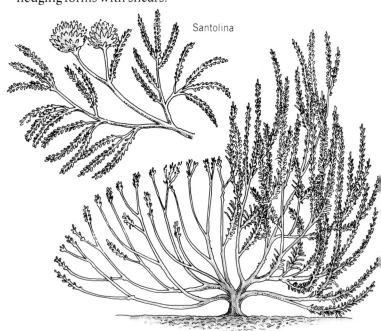

Santolina

SPIRAEA (1 & 2)

S. x *arguta* and other spring-flowering varieties should be cut back to new shoots after flowering. *S.* x bumalda and other summer-flowering varieties are cut back hard to within 7 cm (3 in) of ground level in spring.

SYMPHORICARPOS (SNOWBERRY) (2)

Cut out the oldest and weakest shoots each spring as these will rapidly be replaced by new growth from the base.

SYRINGA (LILAC) (2)

Dead-heading and sucker removal is usually all that is needed. If space is limited or bushes are old or overgrown, cut back hard in April to within 76 cm (2½ ft) of ground level.

ULEX (GORSE) (2)

Cut out the previous year's growth after flowering and thin out any crowded growth. Tall, lanky plants can be cut down to within 15 cm (6 in) of ground level in March.

VIBURNUM (2)

Remove some of the oldest wood every year or two, cutting back to a strong shoot as low down as possible. Do this after flowering except for those grown for their fruits

WEIGELA (2)

Remove the previous year's shoots after flowering to encourage the growth of strong new shoots from lower down the plant. On mature plants cut out some of the old wood each year.

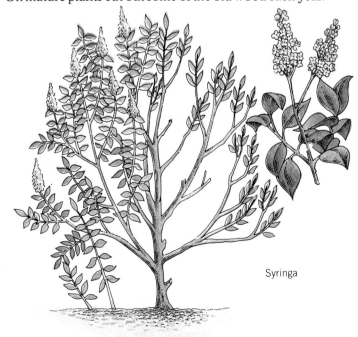

Syringa

CLIMBERS & WALL PLANTS

The pruning guidelines for established climbing plants are exactly the same as those for shrubs. As before, the timing is dictated by the method of flowering, i.e. on the current season's growth, the previous year's growth, or on spurs. With climbers, however, the amount of space available may be critical.

Climbers which are planted to grow through trees are generally best left unpruned, both for practical purposes and safety reasons. Climbers which are planted against walls or fences should be tied in to a system of horizontal wires and the early growths trained in to a fan shape.

Supporting canes are first tied to the wires and the shoots in turn are tied to the canes. Lateral shoots can be tied in to the wires. As the wall or fence area becomes more densely covered some thinning may be necessary, particularly if the growth is uneven. Try to keep the base of the plant well furnished with branches. Vigorous, self-supporting climbers such as clematis must be trained initially as it is difficult to remove the clinging growth once it has a hold. The young shoots of Ivies (Hedera) also need training against their supporting fence or wall.

Key – Group 1 – Flower on the current season's growth
Group 2 – Flower on the previous season's growth
Group 3 – Flower on spurs

Hedera canariensis 'Variegata'.

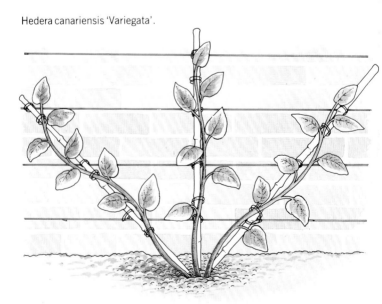

CLEMATIS (1 & 2)

Clematis can be divided into two groups, those that flower in spring and early summer on the previous year's shoots and those that flower in late summer and early autumn on growth made the same year.

Spring and early summer flowering Clematis include the following: *C. montana*, *C. macropetala*, *C.* 'Nelly Moser', *C.* 'Vyvyan Pennell', *C.* 'The President' and *C.* 'Lasurstern'.

These should be pruned immediately the flowers are over. Remove as much of the flowered growth as possible, and thin out any tangled wood and shoots. If varieties in this group get out of hand they can be cut back very hard as they start into growth in spring, although the flowers for that year will be lost.

Late summer and early autumn flowering Clematis include *C.* x *jackmanii*, *C.* 'Ville de Lyon', *C.* 'Ernest Markham', *C.* 'Hagley Hybrid', *C.* 'Henryi', *C.* 'Comtesse de Bouchaud'.

These can be cut back hard in spring just as growth is beginning. If the plants are left unpruned, or only shortened slightly, the flowers will mainly appear high up on the plant leaving the lower stems bare. Cutting shoots to various lengths, from 15 cm (6 in) to 90 cm (3 ft), will ensure coverage of a greater height of wall.

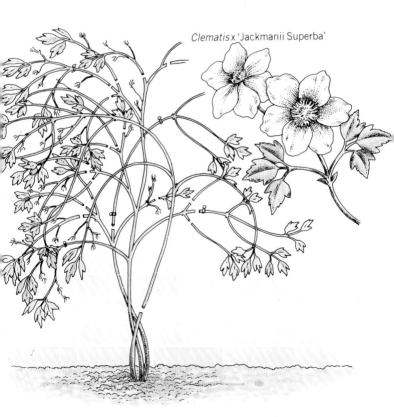

Clematis x 'Jackmanii Superba'

WISTERIA (3)

Wisterias are vigorous growers and should not be planted in a confined space where they will have to be unnaturally restricted. However, if left completely unpruned they will soon reach the roof of the house and dislodge the tiles with their invasive shoots, causing considerable damage. In spite of being such a vigorous plant, Wisterias can sometimes be very slow starters. Cut the young plant back by about half on planting to encourage strong basal growth, from which to train the basic framework. Spur pruning is then practised and the lateral shoots are cut back to 15 cm (6 in) in July except for any shoots needed to extend the framework.

In winter these shoots should be cut back to two buds to encourage the plant to produce large drooping racemes of flowers in the following spring.

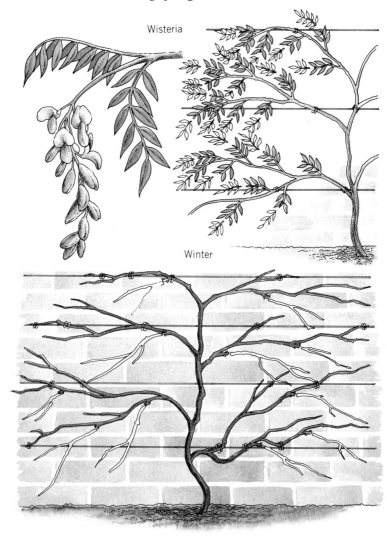

Wisteria

Winter

SHRUBS AS WALL PLANTS
In the same way as climbers, wall plants should have a good basic framework of branches which spread evenly over the allotted space. If the plant has a strong leader this should be cut back by one third every spring to encourage the development of side branches and the new leader should be trained in vertically; selected laterals can also be treated the same way. Plants with a bushy growth should have some well spaced shoots selected as the basic framework. These shoots should be shortened by about one third in the same way to encourage an even coverage.

When the plant reaches the edge of the space allowed, it must be controlled, and this is especially true of wall- and fence-trained plants. Once the plant grows higher than the wall it is liable to be buffeted by the wind and the branches either broken off or badly damaged. Do not be tempted to cut the protruding branches at wall height. Instead remove the branch lower down the plant, making the cut just above a good lateral shoot to help preserve the natural appearance of the plant.

Ceanothus

CLIMBER GUIDE

AMPELOPSIS

No regular pruning is necessary if this climber is given plenty of space to begin with. To control the size, cut back side shoots to two or three buds of the basic framework in January. If pruned later in the year, bleeding is likely.

CAMPSIS (TRUMPET CREEPER) (1)

When the basic branch structure has been formed, cut back the previous year's growth to three buds in spring, and remove any frost-damaged growth. Shoots needed to extend coverage should be cut by a third to encourage flowering side shoots.

HEDERA (IVY)

These popular evergreen climbers have two forms of growth: the juvenile or runner growth with aerial roots, and the adult growth which bears the flowers and fruits. Adult growth should be pruned in March to maintain the shape. Cut back hard any shoots growing away from the wall. *Never* allow Hedera to grow over window frames, gutters or roofs.

HYDRANGEA (2)

Like Hedera, the young shoots will cling to the wall but older shoots will not. Cut back flowering shoots hard in April.

JASMINUM (JASMINE) (1)

J. officinale is a very vigorous plant needing plenty of space and good support. If necessary, thin out any shoots after flowering in late summer.

Jasminum

LONICERA (HONEYSUCKLE) (1 & 2)
The common honeysuckle, *L. periclymenum,* flowers on the previous year's growth so any pruning should be done just after flowering, but try to retain the natural form of the plant. A few varieties, such as 'Serotina', flower much later in the summer on the current season's growth, and these should be cut back hard to the basic framework in winter if necessary.

PARTHENOCISSUS (VIRGINIA CREEPER)
Very vigorous, so some cutting back may be needed in winter in order to keep the plant under control. In particular prevent it from clogging gutters, dislodging slates and obscuring windows.

POLYGONUM (RUSSIAN VINE) (1)
P. baldschuanicum is a wildly rampant climber. Only plant it where it has space to grow 3 m (10 ft) a year. Pruning should be done in March.

SOLANUM (POTATO VINE) (1)
Cut out any frost-damaged shoots of *S. crispum* and *S. jasminoides* in spring and remove any weak and unnecessary growth. The previous year's shoots should be reduced by half.

VITIS
Once the basic structure is established, cut back the previous year's growth in winter if necessary.

Lonicera

TREES

TREE TRAINING   Trees are the largest and most important plants in the garden and because of their long lifespan, it is important that they should be well shaped from the beginning. Pruning, particularly in the early stages, is a vital factor in forming a well shaped tree.

Basically, there are two types of tree: the feathered tree and the standard tree. The feathered tree has branches almost down to ground level, while the standard tree has a clear trunk of about 1.5–1.8 m (5–6 ft) before the first branch. In both cases the aim should be for a strong evenly spaced branch structure.

If feathered trees are planted round the edge of a lawn, the lowest branches may be removed (always cut them flush with the main trunk). This not only makes grass cutting easier, but the lower branches are not damaged by the lawn mower.

Standard Tree

Feathered Tree

A feathered tree can be trained as a standard with a central leader, by removing the lower branches and leaving a bare bole of about 1.5–1.8 m (5–6 ft). Instead of cutting out the leader and encouraging the side branches, the leader is left in place and only weak or crossing laterals are removed.

Care should be taken not to allow a double leader to develop and any lateral growing vertically and competing with the leader should be cut out.

The overhanging branches of trees planted near pavements or driveways sometimes cause problems, and although it is easier, don't just clip back the offending branches along the boundary but cut them back to a lateral well within the head of the tree. This will not only help to maintain the tree's basic shape and informal appearance but will also give you a clearer passageway.

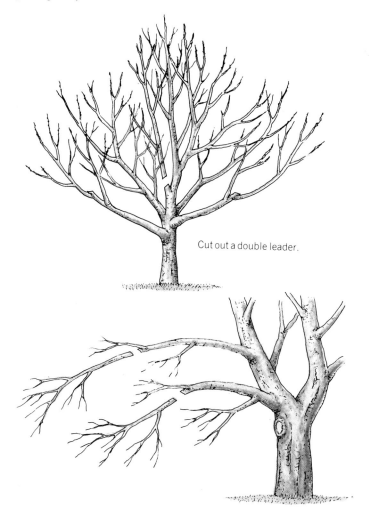

Cut out a double leader.

SMALL SCALE SURGERY

Repairs When it comes to tree surgery the first rule is not to be too ambitious. Scrambling about high in the branches of an old tree is sheer folly and could have a disastrous end. If major work is necessary, for example, the felling of dead elms, it is much easier *and* safer, to call in an expert. There are, however, some tasks that can safely be undertaken by the gardener, and in particular routine work on dwarf fruit trees and the less vigorous flowering trees which are suitable for the small garden.

Broken branches are one of the commonest troubles and can arise from storm damage, a misdirected football, or maybe a child swinging on a thin branch. Sadly it is usually a waste of time to try and splice the two pieces together. The majority of these breaks are usually rough tears which trap water and cause the affected part to rot. It is far better to remove the damaged wood and cut back to a lower branch or shoot which can be trained in as a replacement.

Suckers These should always be removed as they are both unsightly and an unnecessary drain on the tree's resources. Cherries, limes, and various weeping trees are particularly prone to suckering. Always remove suckers as close as possible to their point of origin.

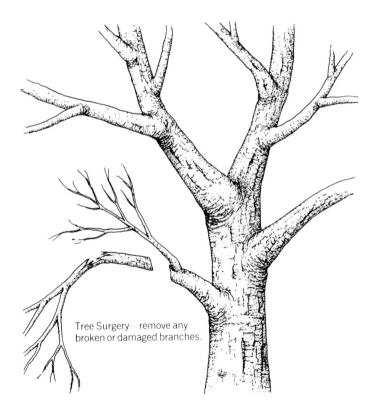

Tree Surgery — remove any broken or damaged branches.

THINNING A DENSE TREE

Deciduous trees planted close to windows sometimes cast too much shade and may need thinning. Although it is easier to see in summer, by the amount of shade cast, which branches need removing, an even branch structure is more easily attained if pruning is done in winter when the tree has shed its leaves. Perhaps the best plan is to mark in summer the branches which seem to need removal and then to do the pruning in the winter when the overall branch structure can be seen.

Thinning should only be attempted on small trees providing the necessary work is easily managed. For larger specimens, always enlist the help of a specialist – it is safer for both you and the tree. On a smallish tree, up to half the branches can be removed without undue harm, but do make sure that all wounds are sealed with protective wound paint as soon as the cuts are made. Conifers are best left unpruned and unthinned, although some varieties such as x *Cupressocyparis leylandii* will stand clipping.

TOPIARY

The art of training evergreens such as yew and box into unnatural shapes belongs more to the days of grand houses and formal gardens, although many exotic creations can also be seen throughout the countryside, often in cottage gardens. The animals or birds are made by tying selected branches to a wire framework, and by careful clipping. Any branches which would ruin the shape are removed completely. With care and patience the most fantastic shapes can be created, but they do need constant attention if their neat shape is to be retained.

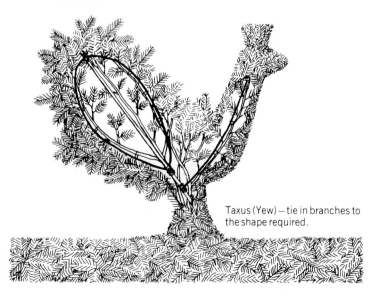

Taxus (Yew) – tie in branches to the shape required.

HEDGES

A good hedge, whatever its type and use, is formed largely by its early training. For example, if you allow a hedge to reach its required height too quickly, without cutting it back, it will soon become bare at the base and thin in the middle. Constant cutting back encourages the thick bushy growth which makes the hedge an impenetrable barrier.

With the exception of conifers, cut back all hedging plants by half after planting. Upright growing subjects like privet (Ligustrum) and snowberry (Symphoricarpos) can be cut back by half or even more, while those tending to form a trunk, like beech (Fagus) and hornbeam (Carpinus) should be cut back by only a third.

In the following year trim privet and snowberry lightly in midsummer and in winter cut back by about a third. Thereafter trim to shape as required. Beeches should not be touched again until the following winter when all growth can be cut back by a quarter or a third. Trimming to shape can begin in the following year.

Flowering hedges are best treated informally, that is left to grow freely, and should be cut at the appropriate pruning time, depending on their flowering season.

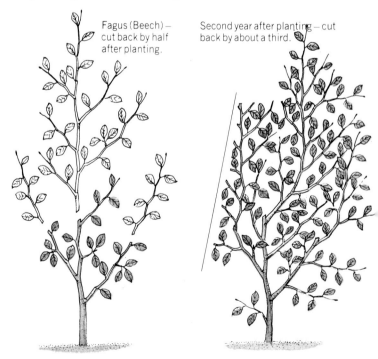

Fagus (Beech) – cut back by half after planting.

Second year after planting – cut back by about a third.

Conifer hedging should be allowed to grow until the required height is reached. The top is then cut 15 cm (6 in) below the final height and the sides lightly trimmed.

Established hedges should be trimmed so that they are wider at the base, tapering slightly to a flat top. This helps keep the base well covered, and makes the hedge more resistant to snow and strong winds.

Large-leaved hedging plants should always be trimmed with secateurs, for if the leaves themselves are cut, not only will they look ugly but the edges will turn brown and die. Electric or hand trimmers are, of course, fine for small-leaved plants, and the more often such a hedge is clipped, the more formal the appearance.

Small hedges which are used more to mark the edges of borders, rather than the edges of gardens, can be cut square, but no hedge should ever be cut with the top wider than the bottom.

CHEMICAL PRUNING

Cutting hedges, especially long ones, can be a tiresome business. Vigorous hedges like Privet are especially troublesome and a useful labour-saving device is a chemical which can be sprayed on the hedge to suppress the growth. Although the apical bud growth is suppressed, the spray encourages all the lateral buds to break slowly so that the hedge grows less but becomes more bushy. The hedge is cut normally and a short time after the growth regulator is sprayed on. The slow-growth effect of the chemical lasts for a whole season.

Berberis x stenophylla — clip into shape immediately after flowering.

Before

After

HEDGE GUIDE

BERBERIS (BARBERRY)

Berberis x *stenophylla* in particular makes a good semi-formal flowering hedge. If it is clipped over immediately after flowering it may flower again in the autumn. Other varieties should also be trimmed after flowering.

BUXUS (BOX)

Clip closely in July or August with hand shears or electric clippers. Straggly hedges may be cut back hard in May.

CHAMAECYPARIS (CYPRESS)

C. lawsoniana varieties. Young hedges should have the leader cut out 15 cm (6 in) below the required height. Lightly clip into shape annually in August.

COTONEASTER

C. simonsii is the common hedging plant and is best treated informally. Thin out any straggly growth after fruiting.

X CUPRESSOCYPARIS (LEYLAND CYPRESS)

The fast-growing x *Cupressocyparis leylandii* is often used as a windbreak or for screening. However, if it is not pruned regularly each August, it will rapidly grow too big for the average garden.

FAGUS (BEECH)

Established hedges can be cut back in August, preferably with secateurs. It retains its brown leaves all winter.

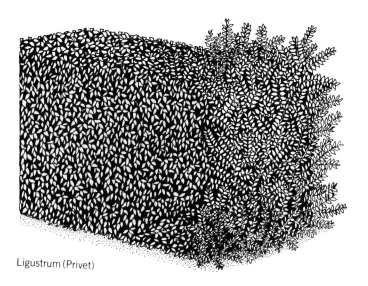

Ligustrum (Privet)

GRISELINIA
Prune with secateurs in July, or if a more formal appearance is needed use shears.

ILEX (HOLLY)
Hedges should be trimmed annually in August. If the hedge is sparse or overgrown it can be cut back very hard. Cut the sides in successive years, and the top in the third.

LIGUSTRUM (PRIVET)
Clip regularly from May to August. Cut out any reverted green shoots from the golden and variegated varieties.

LONICERA
Clip *L. nitida* every month between May and August. Can become bare at the base in which case cut it down hard to 15 cm (6 in) in early summer.

PRUNUS
P. laurocerasus, the cherry or common laurel, is best pruned with secateurs in July. *P. lusitanica*, or Portugal laurel, can be clipped, also in July.

TAXUS (YEW)
Trim annually in August, although for a specially smooth finish, it can be clipped more frequently.

THUJA
Clip once a year in August.

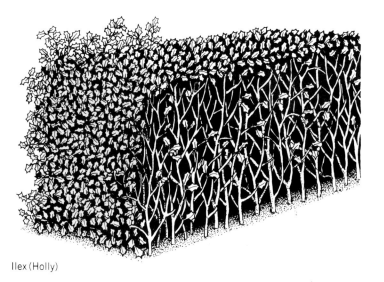

Ilex (Holly)

HOUSEPLANTS

FOLIAGE PLANTS Many houseplants are left to grow unchecked, yet a little judicious pruning, particularly in the spring, improves their appearance enormously. Poor light during the winter months encourages long weak growth, especially if the plants are kept in warm, centrally heated rooms where the heat encourages them to grow, but not to grow well.

Most foliage plants will benefit if their shoots are shortened in the spring to encourage the development of side shoots, and many can also be pinched back during the growing season as well.

Climbing and trailing varieties can be trained over arches or round window frames, and in this case will need some formative training and tying in of shoots.

Philodendron scandens — remove long spindly growth in spring.

FOLIAGE PLANT GUIDE

ADIANTUM (MAIDENHAIR FERN)
Any shrivelled fronds should be cut out at soil level using a pair of pointed scissors. Plants can be cut down entirely in spring as new fronds start to uncurl.

BEGONIA
Remove dead leaves. Tall varieties can be shortened in spring.

CHLOROPHYTUM (SPIDER PLANT)
Opinions vary, some like to remove the shoots carrying the 'babies', others like to leave them to develop.

COLEUS (FLAME NETTLE)
Pinch out flower buds for bushy growth. In February shorten all growths of *C. blumei* if grown on for a second year.

FATSHEDERA
The stems can be shortened as necessary in spring.

FICUS (RUBBER PLANT)
F. elastica, the India rubber plant, is best left unpruned. If it becomes too tall or straggly, air layer the top and then cut the plant back hard. Encourage bushy growth of other species by pinching out the tops as necessary.

Adiantum — cut down to soil level in spring.

GREVILLEA (SILKY OAK)
Retain the central leader as long as possible. If the plant becomes too large, cut it back hard and train a new leader.

MONSTERA (SWISS CHEESE PLANT)
Best left to grow bigger and bigger but it can be cut back if space runs out.

PEPEROMIA
In spring pinch out the growing points of varieties with long stems to encourage bushier growth.

PHILODENDRON
Pinch out the growing tips of *P. scandens* to encourage bushy growth and bigger leaves. Cut back spindly shoots in spring.

PILEA (ALUMINIUM PLANT)
Pinch out the growing tips in spring, or the plant will become leggy and less attractive.

RHOICISSUS (GRAPE IVY)
Encourage bushy growth by stopping the growing points of *R. rhomboidea* and then letting it grow. If it becomes too large, cut it back by a half or even more in spring. *Cissus antarctica* should be treated in the same way.

Monstera – plants which become too large can be cut back or air layered.

FLOWERING PLANTS

The pruning guidelines for flowering plants in the home and greenhouse are exactly the same as those for pruning hardy shrubs. The timing will depend on the flowering habit of the plant, and the aim is to encourage the production of flowering wood. For example, Impatiens, which flowers on the current season's growth, should be cut hard in spring.

Flowering plants suffer even more in houses than foliage plants and it is a good idea, unless you buy them and discard them after flowering, to keep them in a greenhouse for most of the year. They can be brought into the house for flowering and will be much happier for this pampered treatment.

FLOWERING PLANT GUIDE

APHELANDRA (ZEBRA PLANT)
Cut out the dead flower head to a pair of healthy side shoots for flowering later.

AZALEA
When the flowers fade remove them and at the same time trim back any straggling shoots to an even shape.

BEGONIA
Cut back in spring by as much as half to encourage a bushy habit and floriferous growth.

BELEPERONE (SHRIMP PLANT)
Cut back the main stems of *B. guttata* by about half each spring, otherwise the plant will produce long weak growth.

Impatiens — cut back old plants in the spring.

BOUGAINVILLEA
Prune back lateral shoots to two or three buds and shorten leaders by about a third. Remove any weak or diseased shoots.

CAMPANULA (ITALIAN BELLFLOWER)
All the shoots of *C. isophylla* should be cut back hard after flowering.

CITRUS
No pruning is usually necessary, but if the plant loses its shape, cut back all shoots by about half in spring.

CLERODENDRUM
C. speciosissimum doesn't usually need pruning, but if the plant becomes straggly, cut back fairly hard in April.

COLUMNEA
When flowering is over, cut back the faded flower stems and thin out any weak or bare shoots.

ERICA (HEATH, HEATHER)
Trim back hard after flowering but don't cut into old wood.

EUPHORBIA (POINSETTIA)
Cut back the stems of *Euphorbia pulcherrima* to about 10 cm (4 in) after flowering, but the plant will still grow quite tall.

Euphorbia — cut back after flowering.

FUCHSIA
All pruning should be done as growth starts in spring. Trailing varieties should be cut back fairly hard. Small bushy varieties should be cut lightly, older, straggly ones need to be cut back hard. Plants trained on a trellis should be cut back to within two buds of the main stems. Dead-head regularly.

HIBISCUS (ROSE OF CHINA)
Cut back hard in March to base of previous year's growth.

HOYA (WAX FLOWER)
Pinch out the growing tips on young plants to encourage more side growth. Any shoots which cannot be trained in should be cut back hard. No dead-heading is necessary.

NERIUM
Shorten flowering shoots and laterals by half after flowering.

PELARGONIUM (GERANIUM)
Cut back by a third to a half in spring. If they are planted out for the summer repeat when plants are lifted in the autumn.

PLUMBAGO
Shorten all shoots by up to two thirds in spring and dead-head when the flowers fade.

SOLANUM (CHRISTMAS CHERRY)
Cut back by half when the fruits have fallen, and pinch back the resulting growth lightly to keep the plant bushy.

Fuchsia — straggly
plants should
be cut back hard.

Pruning Calendar

The times indicated in this pruning calendar are intended as a rough guide only, for the climate can vary by as much as three weeks from one part of the country to another.

JANUARY Overhaul garden equipment and tools. Brush snow off conifers and other evergreens. Remove any damaged or broken branches .

FEBRUARY Complete winter pruning of apples, pears and bush fruits. Remove any dead wood or suckers. Cut autumn fruiting raspberries to ground level.
Start pruning plants grown in the greenhouse.

MARCH Prune established roses. Cut back hard any shrubs grown for their decorative foliage or coloured stems. Any shrubs which need rejuvenating should also be cut back hard. Cut out the old fronds from ferns. Prune Buddleias and other shrubs which flower on the current season's growth.

APRIL Start pruning shrubs which flower on the previous year's growth as the flowers begin to fade. Clip over winter heathers after the flowers fade.

MAY Dead-head Rhododendrons. Remove any rose suckers. Start clipping hedges. Continue pruning spring-flowering shrubs.

JUNE Pinch out growing tips of bedding plants after planting. Pinch out Dahlias and Chrysanthemums as necessary. Continue pruning spring-flowering shrubs. Prune Plum trees.

JULY Thin out Apples if necessary now that the natural 'drop' is over. Prune Cherry trees. Prune Red and White Currants.

AUGUST Dead-head Buddleias and other summer-flowering shrubs plus herbaceous plants and annuals. Summer prune Wisteria, Apples and other fruits. Clip conifer hedges. Prune Cordon Apples and Pears.

SEPTEMBER Thin Grapes. Cut out old Raspberry canes. Prune Peach trees after the fruit is harvested.

OCTOBER Start pruning top fruit after leaf fall. Cut out old canes from blackberries and hybrid berries.

NOVEMBER Cut back Roses and Buddleias by half to prevent wind rock. Start pruning Black Currants and Gooseberries.

DECEMBER Prune Vines. Root prune top fruits and Figs if necessary. Spur back Chaenomeles and Wisteria.

INDEX